T0348389

"A spectacularly well-rounded 1 grounded in creation, centered ᴏⁿ ᵗʰᵉ ᵍᵒˢᵖᵉˡ, ᵃⁿᵈ ᵃᵢᵐᵉᵈ at practical discipleship. Daniels and Reid have written a thoughtful and accessible book that will inspire many to play for the glory of God. I highly commend it to athletes, coaches, fans, or anyone interested in the intersection of faith and sports."

> **JEREMY TREAT,** Pastor for Preaching and Vision, Reality Church LA; Professor of Theology, Biola University; Fellow, The Keller Center for Cultural Apologetics

"Daniels and Reid masterfully address the complex intersection of faith and sports, offering practical wisdom for athletes, coaches, and sports professionals seeking to honor God in their competitive pursuits. As someone deeply involved in preparing the next generation of sports business professionals, I find this book to be an invaluable resource. It's essential reading for anyone wanting to compete with both excellence and godliness in today's sports landscape."

> **DR DARIN W. WHITE,** Samford University / Brock School of Business; Margaret Gage Bush Distinguished Professor; Executive Director, Sports Industry Program

"A must-read for any Christian athlete. Graham and Jonny do a great job of encouraging us back to a foundation of knowing the treasure of Christ and who we are in him. May this bring you restored freedom to play your sport to the best of the abilities God has given you—for his glory and your delight."

> **DEBBIE FLOOD,** Two-Time Olympic Silver Medalist, Quadruple Sculls Rowing, 2004 and 2008

"Sports are an amazing gift from God, but, just like any good gift, they can become an idol in the hearts of sinners. Graham and Jonny do an excellent job of praising the gift while encouraging the reader to do some deep heart-searching. Any athlete, parent, or coach would do well to read this."

JOHN PERRITT, Author, *Time Out! The Gift or God of Youth Sports*; Director of Resources, Reformed Youth Ministries

"This book reinforces my love for God and the ultimate purpose he has for me through my sport. It takes the complexity of it all and formulates it in a way that is relatable to everyone, using the testimonies of successful sporting figures. No matter what stage you are at as a believer or an athlete, this book will give you a deeper understanding of how your faith and sport can be combined to serve God. I highly recommend it!"

KIRANI JAMES, Olympic Gold Medalist, Men's 400m, 2012; Men's 400m World Champion, 2011

"Engaging, enjoyable, perceptive, and full of biblical wisdom and practical relevance. Every sports-loving Christian should read this."

JAMES ROBSON, Principal, Oak Hill Theological College, London

"Graham is someone I trust and someone who has had a great impact on my life and the lives of many others. I've spoken to him on many occasions when I've had to make difficult decisions in my career. He makes time for people, and I think that's because of his faith."

DAVID MOYES, Former EPL Manchester United and West Ham Manager

"This outstanding book accomplishes what so few Christian books do: it is theologically rich, culturally insightful, accessible, well-applied, and heartwarming throughout. Whether you are an elite athlete, a parent of a child who is passionate about sport, a coach, a club player, or a fan, you will find so much to benefit you here."

PETE NICHOLAS, Senior Pastor, Redeemer Presbyterian Church, Downtown, New York

"This book puts you in the mind and heart of the athlete. I would highly recommend this book to those looking for encouragement along their athletic journey, those looking to find the words to encourage a friend or training partner, and those wanting to connect their faith to their sports."

CHRISTIAN TAYLOR, Two-Time Olympic Gold Medalist, Men's Triple Jump, 2012 and 2016; Four-time Triple Jump World Champion

"Sports dominate our cultural landscape. It's a gift, not a god. *Spiritual Game Plan* is a great little book for those who love sports and love Jesus, and want to relate these two loves in an ordered rather than disordered way. Recommended."

DAN STRANGE, Director, Crosslands Forum; Author, *Plugged In* and *Making Faith Magnetic*

"Over the last 40 years, no one I know has given more thought to the relationship between Christianity and sports than Graham Daniels. This gem of a book will help you think rightly in order to play, watch, and enjoy the God-given gift of sports for his glory."

GAVIN PEACOCK, Former EPL Chelsea and Newcastle Midfielder; Author, *A Greater Glory: From Pitch to Pulpit*

"Love sports? This wonderful book can help you enjoy them more as you frame being an athelte in God's big plan for you and the world."

PAUL REES, Lead Pastor, Charlotte Chapel,
Edinburgh, Scotland

"I love this book. Graham and Jonny have filled it with Scripture and insights from Christian athletes and their stories; with sound theology and wise practice; with Christ-centered perspective and plain guidance for players, fans, coaches, and parents. And all this under the banner of God's glory through Christian joy and our joy to his glory. I only wish we had had this book sooner. In our sports-obsessed society, this will help Christians of all ages, all sorts, and all sports."

DAVID MATHIS, Senior Teacher, desiringGod.org;
Pastor, Cities Church, Saint Paul, MN;
Author, *A Little Theology of Exercise*

"This book covers so many poignant topics related to winning and losing and how we see ourselves when we're immersed in the sporting world. It shows us that we are more than our achievements and that it's possible to be successful without a medal. Chapter 4 was particularly resounding for me."

NATHAN JONES, Former EPL Southampton Manager;
Charlton Athletic Manager

Spiritual Game Plan

Graham Daniels & Jonny Reid

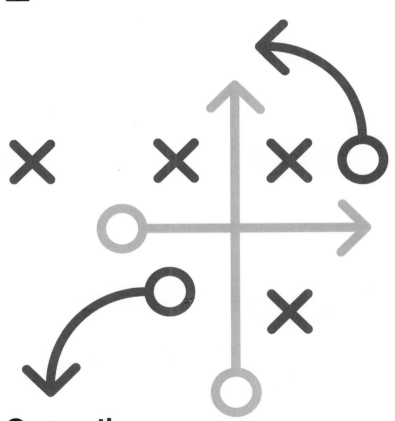

Competing with Joy and Godliness

Spiritual Game Plan: Competing with Joy and Godliness
© Graham Daniels/Jonny Reid 2025

US Edition

Published by:
The Good Book Company

thegoodbook.com | thegoodbook.co.uk
thegoodbook.com.au | thegoodbook.co.nz | thegoodbook.co.in

Cover design by Studio Gearbox | Art direction and design by André Parker

ISBN: 9781802543070 | JOB-008111 | Printed in India

Contents

Introduction

I (Graham) was a professional soccer player when I became a Christian in 1984. (This happened to be the year my team set the all-time record for most successive games without a win, but that's beside the point.) I went to meet my new church leaders to discuss baptism. The conversation went well—until one of them questioned whether it was appropriate for a Christian to work in the highly competitive and commercial world of professional soccer.

It was a good question.

Before I'd formulated a response, one of the other leaders pointed out that being a professional athlete brought many evangelistic opportunities. He accepted that elite sports had several negative aspects but said that the platform provided by being a soccer player potentially countered them, because I could use my (small amount of) fame and status for public evangelism.

The suggestion that the merits of evangelism trumped the defective aspects of professional soccer won the day. The meeting with my church leaders ended well, and the request for baptism was granted. Soon enough I did have opportunities to speak about Jesus at several events, both as the "celebrity" testimony and alongside far more successful athletes. It appeared that you could be a Christian in sports as long as you realized that the point of sports was as a useful platform to evangelize people.

I (Jonny) was not yet born in 1984, and I have never come near to professional level in any sport! But I did grow up sports-obsessed. As soon as I could walk, I had a stick and a ball in my hand. From hockey to cricket to golf, anything that involved a bat and a ball would occupy me for hours (and in the case of cricket, days!). I played competitive sports throughout school. I put my trust in Jesus in my teenage years, and from then on, the two dominant aspects of my life were my faith and my sports. But the two never mixed. It wasn't until I was 17, having played competitive sports for nearly ten years, that I was first challenged by the idea that maybe God had something to say about sports and how I competed.

We are guessing you picked up this book because you love sports (or someone in your family does) and because you also love Jesus. So which of the three approaches we've outlined here do you find yourself most naturally aligning with?

1. Deep down you think sports are probably a waste of time and that proper Christians should spend time doing proper Christian things. Sports are not one of those things, and so you feel a bit guilty about loving them.

2. Sports are a useful vehicle for evangelism. They give a platform for the gospel, and so it's okay to play if you use it to share the gospel.

3. Sports are great, obviously! And you've never really thought about if and how they connect with your faith.

In our experience most Christians take one of these three approaches unless they steer clear of sports altogether (which neither of us can quite imagine doing, but God did make everyone different!). In this book we want to offer you a fourth way of thinking about sports. It's one which starts with God and asks why God would ordain the creation of this thing we call sports. It's a way which shows how sports are a wonderful gift that God can use to play a key role in our growth and maturity as Christians. As we look at the Bible, we'll see a more liberating approach than feeling a bit guilty, a deeper approach than only seeing sports as an evangelistic opportunity, and a better approach than not linking our faith and our sports at all.

To do that we're going spend six chapters looking at what God's word says about sports and how the gospel transforms our thinking about and participation within it. Having established these core principles, the last four chapters of the book will apply them to various different ways of being involved in sports besides simply playing. So please read all of the first six chapters, and then pick and choose the ones at the end that apply to your particular circumstances.

It's fair to say we both *love* sports. Our prayer is that this book will enhance your love for sports too—but also, and more importantly, exponentially increase your love for God.

And in case you're wondering, I (Graham) am no longer the not so proud owner of the record for the longest streak without winning. I'm grateful to the efforts of Derby County of the English Premier League in 2007-2008 for removing that particular accolade from me...

Chapter 1

Why God Made Sports

Sports, at their best, are a source of great joy—and there's a reason for that. In the film *Chariots of Fire*, the 1924 Olympian Eric Liddell says:

> *"I believe God made me for a purpose, but he also made me fast, and when I run, I feel his pleasure."* *

These words reveal why God made a world that includes sports, why so many of us are wired to love them, and why the Bible has much to say about them.

The world of the Bible was an ancient one, but it was also an active one. The apostle Paul, for instance, was clearly familiar with sports and regularly chose to use athletic metaphors for living the Christian life: a race (1 Corinthians 9:24), a fight (1 Timothy 6:12), training (2 Timothy 3:16) and so on.

---

* While he says this in the film, it's not clear if Liddell actually said this in real life. But it captures well his approach to his running.

But to understand what the Bible says about sports, we need to go a bit deeper (and a lot earlier) than the New Testament's use of athletic language. We need to go back to the beginning, to creation. It will seem as if we've stepped away from sports (having only just begun), but as we explore four aspects of God's design and desire for humanity, we'll see how they connect to our sporting life—and how each both explains our love for and increases our joy in sports.

Creativity: *God Is Creative, and Sports Reflects This*

The very first line of the Bible tells us:

In the beginning God created the heavens and the earth. (Genesis 1:1)

Now, just in case you have swept over this familiar sentence without finding it awesome, we are going to stop and see if we can make your jaw drop. Let's consider a slightly later part in the creation story:

God made two great lights—the greater light to govern the day and the lesser light to govern the night. He also made the stars. (Genesis 1:16-17)

Check out those final five words: "He also made the stars." It reads like a throwaway line. Yet scientists estimate there are 200 billion galaxies in the observable universe. To the Creator God, such an awesome act is so easy that it is almost captured as a footnote.

Now look outside the window (or go and find one if you're reading in a windowless room) and look at the different things you can see. If you can see a tree, then it is one of over 73,000 different species, and trees are one group within the 380,000 or so species of plant that God chose to create. Each was intricately designed by the same God who made the stars. God is innately and wonderfully creative, and designed a vast, ordered and perfect world.

However, in a sense, God left some work to be done on his behalf. As the Bible teacher and author Nancy Guthrie says, "Eden was unspoiled but also unfinished."[1] This is where the story of human creativity begins:

> *Then God said, "Let us make mankind in our image, in our likeness, so that they may rule over the fish in the sea and the birds in the sky, over the livestock and all the wild animals, and over all the creatures that move along the ground." (Genesis 1:26-27)*

Humans are God's "image." To understand what this means, it is helpful to know that the book of Genesis, like the rest of the Old Testament, was mostly written in Hebrew. The Hebrew word translated as "image" can also be translated as "idol" or "statue"—the word means a visible representation of an invisible being. Therefore, while many religions place statues of gods in temples so that worshipers can "see" their god, Genesis makes it plain that humans don't need to build stone images because we are made as God's living images. "As a mirror reflects, so a man should reflect God ... in man God is to become visible on earth."[2]

One implication of being God's image on earth is

captured in God's job description for humanity in Genesis 2:15:

> *The LORD God took the man and put him in the Garden of Eden to work it and take care of it.*

Once again, to grasp the wonder of what God is doing, we need to unpack the sentence. The original Hebrew word translated here as "work" can also be translated as "service," and it is also often rendered as "worship" in the Old Testament (for instance Exodus 3:12; 8:1; 2 Samuel 15:8; Psalm 102:22).

The relationship between these three words is very important. Work, service and worship are not separate things. We are used to separating at least two of these ideas—"work" and "worship." We typically view "work" as doing your job to earn a living and "worship" as what happens in church buildings.

Genesis does not do this. All kinds of creative enterprises—what we would tend to call activities of "work" or even "leisure"—contribute to the worship of God in the fulfillment of his plan to develop his world. Tim Keller defines "work" as...

> *"... rearranging the raw material of God's creation in such a way that it helps the world in general, and people in particular, thrive and flourish."* [3]

The "creation mandate"—to rule the world under God by working and taking care of it—implies that every creative activity is an opportunity to work in the service of God and is (or should be), therefore, an act of worship. The worship of God is to be found in every aspect of human creativity, including entrepreneurship, engineering, business, the arts, music... and sports.

Sports are full of creation. We're creative in sports when we invent a new shot (like the step-back three-pointer in basketball), when we work out the best way to get the better of our opponent during a game, or even when someone creates a new chant in the stands. God created people with athletic ability to use their sporting talents to work, serve and worship him.

And there's more. God's plan, captured in that job description, was for humanity to riff on God's initial design and extend it. The first man and woman were to extend the Eden that God had made. Whenever we create within God's creation, we are reflecting this God-given role. Sports are an outworking of this; over the centuries, humans have developed numerous sports by taking games and formalizing the rules and rankings. Today, there are millions of people playing hundreds of sports across the globe. To take one example, a Christian, James Naismith, while he was studying at the YMCA's International Training School, wanted to create a game that would connect sports and faith by promoting character traits like teamwork and creativity while minimizing the use of physical violence that was found in other sports. The result was basketball.

The invention of any sport, with the imagination required to take an initial kernel of an idea and bring it to an ordered and bounded form for mass participation, is itself reflecting the kind of world that God created.

Sports bring out our God-given creativity. Designing or playing is an opportunity to develop God's good creation and fulfill our job description to work, serve and worship God in the world he has made.

Community: *God Has Always Been in Community, and Sports Are About Relationships*

In the creation story, God says:

> *Let us make mankind in our image, in our likeness.*
> *(Genesis 1:26)*

God speaks about himself as "us"—as plural rather than singular. As the Bible unfolds, it becomes clear that this is because God has never been on his own, but has always been three-in-one. "You loved me before the creation of the world" (John 17:24) is how Jesus, God the Son, describes his eternal relationship with God the Father. This is why we can say that "God is love" and that God was love before there was any human to love. This love from eternity flows down to, and should flow out from, us:

> *Dear friends, let us love one another, for love comes from God. Everyone who loves has been born of God and knows God. Whoever does not love does not know God, because God is love. (1 John 4:7-8)*

God's design for humanity is to build loving community that reflects his own nature. That's why God says:

> *It is not good for the man to be alone. I will make a helper suitable for him. (Genesis 2:18)*

From the beginning, the mandate to develop God's world involved men and women teaming up to look after his creation. This teamwork is seen at its most basic level in the way new humans are made.

It is deeply human to have relationships—to give and receive love. We need friends, and we need family. We all know this. Of course, being alone is fine, and it sometimes keeps us sane! But to be lonely is terribly distressing, and to feel always alone is even worse.

At its best, sports are deeply communal. Think about the bonds sports create—the exhilaration of a great moment in a team sport when you get to be one individual contributing to a shared victory, or in an individual sport when you win a race and your coach is there to see it, or a time when you look into the crowd or around at the finish line and see someone who loves you, cheering you in.

Sports, even when they are most individualistic, are always a team affair.

Michael Jordan, while involved in a team sport, transcended his team and his sport. Yet, despite his own unrivaled talent, he recognized that he couldn't play without his team, especially his great friend Scottie Pippen:

> *"I didn't win without Scottie Pippen, and that's why I consider him my best teammate of all time. He helped me so much in the way I approached the game, in the way I played the game. Whenever they speak Michael Jordan, they should speak Scottie Pippen."* [4]

Rory McIlroy, a golfer who so often is playing for himself, has often spoken of how much he enjoys the team golf of the Ryder Cup:

> *"It is the most special and unique golf tournament we have, period. There's nothing better than celebrating a win with your teammates."* [5]

Of course, for Christians the primary community is to be found in the church. But, given we're created for community, we can embrace the joy of sporting togetherness too—and we can understand why those who don't follow Jesus so often long for, and even live for, that team or team community. Our Creator designed some of us to make the world a friendlier, happier and more loving place by enjoying our athletic abilities together. Sports, when played in this way, allow us to experience something that humanity has been hardwired both to need and to enjoy—true relationship, deep community.

Delight: *God Delights in Creation and Makes Us to Delight in Sports*

God delighted in creating the world. When God threw 200 billion galaxies into space, that was not just an example of his outrageous creativity but also of his delight and playfulness in creating.

Proverbs 8:30-31 illustrates God's exuberance, joy and delight in the act of creation. The writer of Proverbs introduces us to the person of "Wisdom," who seems to be a poetic picturing of the second Person of the Trinity, the Son. And in Proverbs, Wisdom says:

> *I [Wisdom] was filled with delight day after day,*
> *rejoicing always in his [God's] presence,*
> *rejoicing in his [God's] whole world*
> *And delighting in the human race.*

The sense of divine delight in making the world is also captured in Psalm 104:

> *The LORD wraps himself in light as with a garment;*
> *he stretches out the heavens like a tent and lays the*
> *beams of his upper chambers on their waters.*
> *He makes the clouds his chariot and rides on the wings*
> *of the wind.*
> *He makes winds his messengers, flames of fire his*
> *servants. (v 2-4)*

Note the number of metaphors that capture the sheer joy God had in creating. And since human beings are made in the image of God, we are wired to reflect his delight in and enjoyment of the world. God has provided abundance and joy to his creatures:

> *And the LORD God commanded the man, "You are free*
> *to eat from any tree in the garden; but you must not*
> *eat from the tree of the knowledge of good and evil, for*
> *when you eat from it you will certainly die."*
>
> *(Genesis 2:16-17)*

We tend to focus on the prohibition. But don't miss that the dominant perspective here is one of extravagance. Humanity was to enjoy the world and could eat from "any tree" except just one. God alone could set the moral boundaries of right and wrong; there was only one referee, and it wasn't Adam or Eve! But beyond this crucial limitation, there was huge freedom to express ourselves in our creativity, relationships and enjoyment of life.

Proverbs 8:31 specifically emphasizes God's "delighting in mankind." The pastor Jeremy Treat writes:

> *"Like a father who builds a sandbox for his children, God is honored and takes joy when his sons and daughters delight in his workmanship. The world, as it has been said, is the theatre of God's glory but it is also the playground for God's goodness."* [6]

Sports are one of the ways in which we can delight in our bodies and our world. Psalm 19:4-5 compares the feeling of a victorious athlete with a bridegroom on his honeymoon—both total physical and emotional satisfaction:

> *In the heavens God has pitched a tent for the sun.*
> *It is like a bridegroom coming out of his chamber,*
> *like a champion rejoicing to run his course.*

The Bible could not offer much higher praise for the joy to be found in sports than that!

For some people, playing sports draws them really close to God. As you're excited as you leave work on a Tuesday night and head to meet your friends for a pick-up game, or when you go for a run and feel the breeze in your hair, the delight you feel is a gift from God—and when we recognize this, it can draw us closer to him. Every gift we receive as a gift helps point us to the giver. Every race, every game, every competition is an opportunity to experience again the joy that comes from doing something God designed every athlete to love.

British rower Anastasia Chitty captures this idea when she speaks of her sport:

"There's no more special place to me than being on the water. It's my happy place. It's my vision of paradise! The closest thing on earth for me to paradise is being out on the river, with the sun out, in my boat."[7]

Sports are a gift from God to bring us pleasure and joy. God has given you permission—in fact, encouragement—to take delight in using your created body in this created world to run and jump and kick and tackle, and to enjoy it all as a good gift from him. The Christian can take more delight, not less, in their sports than anyone else.

Glory: *God Is to Be Glorified, and We Do That by Finding Our Joy in Him*

Sports were made to give us joy—but we were made to find our ultimate joy in the God who created us with our athletic gifts. The ultimate purpose of humanity is to glorify God, for as the Creator, he is uniquely worthy of receiving glory and praise from his creatures:

... everyone who is called by my name,
whom I created for my glory,
whom I formed and made. (Isaiah 43:7)

We recognize in sports that praise should be given when it is due. Think about it this way—when someone wins a race in a motorsport or track and field, they get to stand at the top of the podium and receive a medal. They deserve this because they have won. It would be odd (and controversial!) if the fourth-placed finisher tried to stand on top of the podium and share or steal the glory due only to the winner.

When someone does something praiseworthy, it's right that they receive praise and right for them to accept that praise. It makes sense that Michael Jordan has won five MVPs and LeBron James four. It makes sense that the best players get picked in All-Star teams or appear on the walls of clubhouses.

God is always and only praiseworthy in all that he does. It would be odd—wrong, in fact—for us not to continually and always give him praise, or for him not to accept it. As creatures, in his world, our ultimate purpose is to glorify God.

And we are able to glorify God whether we win or lose. If you spend any time on social media or listening to postgame interviews, it is easy to find athletes and coaches giving God glory when they win—but we rarely hear such sentiments when they lose. Yet giving glory to God has nothing to do with sporting success or failure.

Shelly-Ann Fraser-Pryce is one of the most successful sprinters of all time, winning three Olympic golds and ten World Championship titles for Jamaica. She also follows Jesus and understands that God's glory isn't related to her success:

> "A lot of persons would believe that if you don't win, God is not there. But he is always there. It does not matter if I win or lose. Just to be able to stand on the line and know that I am a child of God makes me

special and makes me able to say, 'Okay, whatever I am doing today is for him'. And I hope that by me running, he'll get the glory and he'll enjoy it as much as I'm enjoying it. When I run, the first thing I tell myself is this: 'I hope he is pleased with my worship, for running is my worship—my way of worshiping him because he has given me the talents.'" [8]

We give God glory by finding our deepest satisfaction and joy in how much he has done for us as our Creator and loving Father. We are invited as well as commanded to "take delight in the LORD" (Psalm 37:4). There is an inextricable link between giving God glory and finding huge joy in being thoroughly satisfied in him. To echo the pastor John Piper's much-repeated saying, "God is most glorified in us when we are most satisfied in him."

Let's use a sporting analogy to think about this. Imagine a trainer works with an injured athlete to get them back competing at the highest level again. When the athlete can compete, they feel great joy and give great thanks to the trainer. And the trainer is glorified by the athlete being back on the track, competing once more.

Tom Brady, arguably the greatest quarterback of all time, understood this. His knee injury in 2008 could have ended his career. He missed the season, but returned to win more Super Bowls and MVP awards. When he spoke about his return, he said, "I'm excited about the work and all the wonderful people who've helped me … I'm the most well-taken-care-of knee patient in history. I'm very, very fortunate." [9] Imagine the joy and sense of satisfaction that those "wonderful people" must have felt to see Brady back on the field. Brady's greatness was their delight.

This is a glimpse of the reason why God created us: we are created to glorify him, and he gets glory when we are filled with pleasure and joy at what he has done and is doing for us.

So, you can give God glory by rejoicing in your God-given athletic gifts, confident that he delights in showing his overwhelming love in and for you as you compete. His attitude towards you does not change according to your performance or the final score. Instead, he is a God of perfect love, giving us sporting gifts by which we can win or lose and find that in both scenarios, we can appreciate his awesome love for us.

Gavin Peacock, the former EPL player who was captain of both Chelsea and Newcastle, captures this brilliantly when he describes how becoming a Christian changed his view of his sport:

> "I understood what life is about. I understood what [soccer] is about. I could now see [it] as the gift of God—even as a necessary overflow of being created in the image of God. So, then I would see going out there on a Saturday as a display of the wisdom of God in the beauty of sport. So, then [there is a] responsibility to steward those gifts for the glory of God."[10]

Born to Play

Eric Liddell found pleasure in God as he competed in his sport. What about you?

Stop now and think about the sports you love.

Think about where you find joy in them and how you can experience them as an act of worship. Ponder the community and the creativity seen in those sports.

And stop and give God praise for this wonderful gift.

Sports are something God cares about.

Sports are something you can truly enjoy as a Christian.

Sports are something that has to do with God and your relationship with him—in fact, they have everything to do with him.

The wonder of the sporting life is that it is God's purpose to use our talents and relationships to find a lifelong joy, as we compete with others, with God at the center of our lives.

And yet... sports don't always seem to work like that.

Chapter 2

Foul Play

I (Jonny) was playing indoor field hockey against our local rivals in the final of the annual tournament, in front of a small but vocal crowd filled with my friends.

We were losing.

I was getting more and more frustrated as our opponents edged further ahead and our home crowd fell silent. We'd hit the post twice. We'd seen a penalty saved. We'd had a player sent to the penalty box. This was not going how I'd imagined it the night before.

Eventually my frustration boiled over. I went one on one with their goalkeeper, and as he won the ball I slid to the ground and landed on top of him. In an instant, without thinking, my I slapped him on the top of his helmet (a definite no-no in hockey). Everyone in the sports hall saw, except the umpire. But it only took one look at my coach to know I was about to be substituted.

I'd dreamed of lifting the trophy and of basking in the glory of my friends' praises. Instead, I was trudging off before the end. The loss of my dream had led to an overspill of anger and aggression. And once it was done, there was no way to undo it.

If you've played sports for any period of time, I would bet that you have similar stories you can think of right now.

We've seen how sports bring joy and strengthens relationships, and is a way in which we can bring glory to God. Sports are a gift from God to humans, but because we humans are far from perfect, we have a tendency to spoil the gift. And that makes our relationship with sports complicated.

Sports are rife with cheating and deception. Our sporting relationships can be ruined by anger and envy. The delight and joy found in sports can be lost in despair and fear, in times of success as well as of failure.

Just as the Bible gives us a reason for the joy we find in sports, it gives us the explanation for the downsides to sports. Again, we need to go back to the beginning (or almost to the beginning).

Glory: *We Use Sports to Bring Ourselves Glory, Not God*

Satan's temptation of Adam and Eve in Genesis 3 was that they could be like God:

The snake said to the woman ... "God knows that when you eat from it [the forbidden tree] your eyes will be opened, and you will be like God, knowing good and evil." (v 5)

Eve and Adam disobeyed God because they wanted to be in charge of the garden and live independently of

God. The result was what is often called the "fall" from God—and one result of it is that the beauty and wonder of the initial creation was broken.

As Genesis develops, we arrive at Babel. The inhabitants of Babel used their creativity to build the biggest tower they could, by innovating through using bricks instead of stones. They were very clear about their purpose for building this tower:

> ... so that we may make a name for ourselves;
> otherwise, we will be scattered over the face of the
> whole earth. (11:4)

They built the tower to maximize their power, show off their magnificence and find safety and security—and to glorify themselves.

We are not so different. We long to construct an identity for ourselves so we can find safety and receive glory. Competitive pride—a desire to earn ourselves praise, whether from others, ourselves or God—inspires most of our work efforts and much of our leisure pursuits in every area of Western society. C.S. Lewis explains in *Mere Christianity* that...

> "Pride is essentially competitive—is competitive
> by its very nature ... Pride gets no pleasure out of
> having something, only out of having more of it than
> the next man. We say people are proud of being rich,
> or clever, or good-looking but they are not. They are
> proud of being richer, or cleverer, or better-looking
> than others."[11]

We can use our talents either with excellence and in

the service and love of others, or so that we might look down on others. This is where pride comes in.

In sports, pride is often viewed as an essential characteristic for any successful athlete to possess. It's seen in the volleyball player who believes she's the best, who knows she's going to win and is said to have a "champion's mentality." It's found in the sprinter who, in a quest to assert his dominance, questions an opponent's credentials and is applauded for playing mind games. At non-elite levels, opponents are arrogantly dismissed or athletes exaggerate past performances to impress new teammates.

Parents of young athletes are not immune to this either. How easy is it to subtly talk up your child's talent and potential in front of other parents as you compare notes on the sidelines? How easy is it to be disappointed in your children when they don't live up to your dreams and expectations?

Pride—a desire for glory—is everywhere in sports. It results in broken relationships, most significantly seen in any form of discrimination. It results in anxiety and obsession, driving us on in unhealthy ways. Pride, though, also affects how we view our standing before God. Athletes regularly cannot grasp the idea of a God whom we do not need to impress and perform for, because it is the opposite of how sports work.

As we saw in the last chapter, God desires that we find our ultimate joy in him, and it is as we do this that he receives the glory that he alone deserves. But it's so easy to misunderstand this. When are athletes most likely to "give God glory"? After they have succeeded.

They're less likely to do so when they receive an injury or are on the end of a crushing defeat. It's a sign that we think God is most pleased with us when we are most successful—that we earn our way to his approval. Which is, of course, a form of pride.

Pride—whether it is factoring God in or not—is what leads to a win-at-all-costs attitude. A key aspect of sports is a good desire to see what we can achieve *as the people we've been created to be*—how fast can *we* go, how high can *we* jump, how well can *we* play? But this desire becomes distorted when it becomes about wanting to reject these limits—to become more than we are. We see this at the elite level (though not only at the elite level) in the prevalence of doping. The original temptation of the serpent was an enticement to be "like God" (Genesis 3:5), and so often the motivation behind doping is a desire to be more than God has made us. We want to make our name great, and to do so we'll step over God's moral boundaries if we need to.

One of the most (in)famous dopers in sporting history is Lance Armstrong. His autobiography was called *It's Not about the Bike*, and in a sense he was telling the truth: his seven Tour de France victories really weren't about the bike.

When Armstrong won his seventh consecutive Yellow Jersey in 2005, he responded to people questioning whether he had doped by saying, "I'm sorry that you can't dream big. I'm sorry you don't believe in miracles."[12] But Armstrong's version of dreaming big was to dream of being something beyond what God had made him to be. His version of "miracles" was to cast off the boundaries that the Creator had imposed, physically and morally. He wanted to be more than he was, rather than being the best of what he was.

It is not just doping, of course. It is cutting the corner. It is tugging a jersey when no one will see. It is deliberately crossing the line before the start. In a thousand small ways, we find it so easy in sports to decide that we will make the rules and that we will strive to be more than God has made us to be.

God has given us great ability *and* he has given us creaturely limitations. Sports at their best are a mutual exploration of those abilities within those limitations, but sports at their worst is when we seek to transcend those limitations and buy into the lie that we can be more than God has made us to be.

Paul in Romans 3 concludes his description of our condition as humans by saying that...

> *all have sinned and fall short of the glory of God.*
>
> *(v 23)*

We were made in God's image to bring him glory and enjoy him. Instead, we naturally join the builders of Babel and live to earn ourselves praise, enjoying the respect or adulation of others. We were created to glorify God—but we live to glorify ourselves.

Delight: *We Find Our Ultimate Joy in Sports, Not in God*

If aliens were to visit our planet, what would they say human beings value most? What would they conclude most excites people?

Well, on any given weekend our extra-terrestrial visitors would see hundreds of thousands of people file into stadiums, sing passionately and cheer on people playing sports. If they observed those spectators during the following week, the visitors would hear multiple reviews of the previous game and excited previews of the next game.

The aliens would see the players involved in entertaining the crowds dedicate hours of their lives—in gyms or on tracks, up mountains or in pools—to training and improving and then posting about their "gains" for others to see. They would hear one of the most celebrated and revered athletes, Cristiano Ronaldo, say, "Without football, my life is worth nothing."[13]

Our interplanetary travelers would surely conclude that the primary source of fulfillment and satisfaction in these people's lives was sports—watching them, playing them, talking about them.

According to Romans 1, rebellion against God includes taking that which is good and turning it into something that is ultimate.

For although they knew God, they neither glorified him as God nor gave thanks to him, but their thinking became futile and their foolish hearts were darkened. Although they claimed to be wise, they became fools and exchanged the glory of the immortal God for images ... they exchanged the truth about God for a lie and worshiped and served created things rather than the Creator—who is for ever praised.
(v 21-25)

Sports are a good gift from God, given to us partly as a means to delight in him, the giver of all good gifts. But...

> *"the human heart takes good things like a successful career, love, material possessions, even family, and turns them into ultimate things. Our hearts deify them as the center of our lives, because, we think, they can give us significance and security, safety and fulfillment, if we attain them."* [14]

If we love sports, then of course, as fallen sinners in a fallen world, we will be tempted to love sports too much: to make of it an idol—a substitute god. We might find it hard to understand how the Israelites in the Old Testament worshiped a golden calf, and yet we're maybe not as far away from them as we might think, as Jeremy Treat has pointed out:

> *"Imagine a modern religion where people worship a golden image (in this case, the [basketball] NBA Finals trophy). They gather regularly at the temple (The Staples Center), where they take up an offering (ticket purchases) and worship with emotive expression (cheering fans). Of course, as with any religious service, they make sacrifices (their time, their money, and often their families). The high priest (the coach) oversees the activities, and those involved have a series of rituals they perform to prepare (team huddles and chest-bumping), all beneath the icons of the saints of old (retired jerseys in the rafters). There are strict programs of discipleship, learning about the gods so they can become like them (which is why they wear their jerseys and buy their shoes)."* [15]

Sports can so easily, and in so many different ways, be used as a god-substitute and become where we look for what is meant to be found in God alone: our joy, our identity, and even our salvation.

Rosie Woodbridge was a competitive ultimate-frisbee player who struggled with exercise addiction. She recognized that this was due to her putting an overemphasis on sports to bring her satisfaction above anything else:

> *"I knew I was training more than my teammates, and often leaving socials early so I could run extra shuttles the next morning. But I just thought they weren't committed enough. When my level of sport required less training, either during the off-season or when I stepped down a level, I still carried on as much as before. I guess I needed it. I needed it because I was insecure about my place in the squad: I needed to be fitter to be better. I needed it because it made me feel good: when life was hard, running made me feel both alive and free. I needed it because I had to obtain and maintain a physique. I needed to exercise to justify my next meal. I needed to exercise to atone for my last meal."* [16]

Whether it's professional athletes seeking their satisfaction in their performance, fans letting their mood be directed by the results of their team, or parents getting angry when their child doesn't perform to their own expectations, it's idolatry.

And since idols never truly satisfy, sports ultimately can't fulfill our greatest longings, simply because they weren't designed to do that. Tom Brady was once interviewed during an undefeated season in which he would win the MVP. He was dating a supermodel and making millions of dollars. Yet he said:

"Why do I have three Super Bowl rings and still think there's something greater out there for me? I mean, maybe a lot of people would say, 'Hey man, this is what it is. I reached my goal, my dream, my life.' Me, I think, 'God, it's got to be more than this.' I mean this can't be what it's all cracked up to be ... And what else is there for me?" [17]

The interviewer asked him, "What's the answer?" Brady responded:

"I wish I knew. I wish I knew." [18]

He could have been echoing the words of the author of Ecclesiastes:

So, I hated life, because the work that is done under the sun was grievous to me. All of it is meaningless, a chasing after the wind. (2:17)

Sports are a gift from God that can bring us joy, and yet, when we allow them to become our god, the joy disappears and it all becomes meaningless.

So, how do you tell if sports are in some way becoming an idol to you? Here are four diagnostic questions we can ask ourselves:

1. Are sports what I think about and talk about more than anything else? When I have nothing else to think about, is it to sports that my mind wanders?

2. When I think about the conversations in which I grow most excited, passionate, or irritated, do those conversations tend to be ones about sports?

3. Do I get *too* passionate about a particular team? Do their wins make me feel euphoric and/or do their losses make me feel empty or angry—not just disappointed, but somewhat depressed?

4. Is my focus on and excitement about a team, or for playing a particular sport, greater than my focus on and excitement about Jesus Christ or my church?

Community: *We Use Sports to Put Ourselves Above Others*

In 1994, figure skater Tonya Harding was accused of arranging for her rival for the Olympic team, Nancy Kerrigan, to be assaulted before the US Olympic trials so that she would be unable to compete. (The story is told in the film *I, Tonya*.) The Latin word from which we get the English "competition" is *competere*, and it means "striving together." If anything epitomized competitiveness gone wrong, it was this story.

If we look at sports at any level we can see that competitiveness gone wrong is rife. The ultra-runner Sabrina Little writes in her book *The Examined Run*:

> "In general, when I am asked whether I am
> competitive, people do not intend to ask whether
> I strive with others; they want to know whether I
> am, to put it plainly, envious ... today, envy is so

*entwined in our cultural imagination of competition
that we have a difficult time conceiving of competition
without it."* [19]

So, instead of positively competing with the aim of helping both our teammates and our opponents perform to the best of their abilities, we frequently use sports to attempt to display our own superiority and serve ourselves:

*"If one were to design a social exercise that tempts
Christians towards sins such as ambition and
jealousy, they couldn't do much better than a
competitive sport."* [20]

Relationships today—in our sporting lives and beyond—are never perfect and are often painful. That, again, is a result of sin and the fall:

*To the woman [God] said,
"I will make your pains in childbearing very severe;
    with painful labor you will give birth to children.
Your desire will be for your husband,
    and he will rule over you." (Genesis 3:16)*

Even the most wonderful, intimate and loving relationships available to humanity now face tensions, stress and pain. Love which was once so perfect is now fractured. We all know this in our own lives. Our fractured relationship with God leads to fractured relationships amongst ourselves.

And we blame each other for this relentlessly. Think about your own life. How often do you put your hand up and say, "My fault" or "Sorry" instead of trying to find someone else to blame—the referee, the other team, the coach? Once more, this tendency among humans started with the first sin:

[God said to the man] "Have you eaten from the tree from which I commanded you not to eat?" The man said, "The woman you put here with me—she gave me some fruit from the tree, and I ate it." Then the Lord God said to the woman, "What is this you have done?" The woman said, "The serpent deceived me, and I ate."
(v 11-13)

Sports cannot escape from the problems our world faces. They reflect our fallen world; they are not an escape from it. Professional sports rightly seek to address issues such as racism and sexism through campaigns like the NFL's Inspire Change initiative or the "SheBelieves" campaign promoted by the US women's national soccer team, but the problem persists, both on and off the field:

"The findings in our report are unequivocal. Racism, class-based discrimination, elitism and sexism are widespread and deep rooted. It's not banter or just a few bad apples. Discrimination is both overt and baked into the structures and processes within cricket." [21]

That was the finding of a report into English cricket in 2022. But it is fair to say that this isn't only a problem in cricket.

God designed sports as a good gift to humanity, to help make the world a better place as we enjoy using our talents and watching others use theirs, in community.

Yet we turn it into a competition for us to trample on others and thrust ourselves forward.

Creativity: *We Use Our Creativity to Serve Ourselves*

Adam and Eve wanted to be like God himself. God had given in abundance and yet, when the devil tempted them to disobey his one instruction—not to eat from the tree of the knowledge of good and evil—they gave in, desiring to be like God and be able to judge good and evil. As a result, God punished Adam and Eve—and this included their work:

> *Cursed is the ground because of you;*
> *through painful toil you will eat food from it*
> *all the days of your life.*
> *It will produce thorns and thistles for you,*
> *and you will eat the plants of the field.*
>
> *(Genesis 3:17-18)*

Adam and Eve's ability to grow and cultivate and create—to reflect God—was cursed. The garden itself would be filled with thorns and thistles; beauty would be broken by ugliness.

We've seen in Genesis 11 how people use their creative talents to serve and worship themselves above God. But that also just leads to frustration. Do you find life frustrating? Do you find loving others difficult? Do you find the constant injuries and frustrations in sports hard? The curse explains why. In sports as in life, we will experience pain, tiredness and conflict. And we will so often be frustrated in our efforts.

This is the problem with those motivational quotes from high-achieving athletes:

"You dream. You plan. You reach. There will be obstacles. There will be doubters. There will be mistakes. But with hard work, with belief, with confidence and trust in yourself and those around you, there are no limits." [22] — *Michael Phelps*

"Luck has nothing to do with it because I have spent many, many hours—countless hours—on the court working for my one moment in time, not knowing when it would come." [23] — *Serena Williams*

But it simply can't be true that you get whatever you want if you work hard! There is truth here—sports contain obstacles, doubters, mistakes and luck. But for 99.9% of athletes, that's it! There are, in fact, limits. Our "moment" usually doesn't come. Most athletes do not achieve all their goals; they don't get to be able to perform how they would like (or if they do, it's only fleeting). We get tired. We get injured. Our bodies break. Despite all our toil, we are frustrated.

These aren't specific divine punishments, as though an injury shows we've sinned in a particular way; as the pastor Sam Allberry puts it, "It is not that one person's suffering is a sign of his or her sin, but that anyone's suffering is a sign of everyone's sin."[24] But our problems are all reminders that this is life in a fallen world and so sports are often not great, are sometimes awful and are never perfect.

And all that points towards something worse than mere frustration or injury—towards something worse even than death itself. We face an existence without any of God's blessings at all. The worst moments in sports or life more widely are just a glimmer of the awfulness of judgment and hell. While we face many of the implications of the curse now, the greatest of them is to come—and in the light of that, our sporting difficulties can sound quite trivial.

Yet there is some hope. There are "thorns and thistles," but God also says, "You will eat the plants of the field" (v 18). Our toil is not entirely fruitless. Life will be both frustrating and fruitful—there will be times when we do see things work as they should: when we see our fitness improve following hard work, when we see the hard work of injury rehabilitation lead to us playing again, when we work hard and achieve our goal. And when we do, we are given a glimpse of the hope to come.

Beauty, Brokenness... and Hope

Here's the thing about sports, as with all areas of life—there is beauty and there is brokenness. There are gold medals and career-ending injuries. And the reason why there are both is because we're made in God's image and we're marred by the fall—because we live in a world created very good but cursed as a result of human sin.

Creation and humanity are wonderful and fallen, and that extends to the playing field, the arena, the court, the track—in how we think about sports, how we love sports, how we watch and talk about sports and how we participate in sports. We get it wrong when we don't see that it's flawed. We get it wrong when we see it as only flawed. And, as we're about to see, we get it wrong when we forget that nothing is beyond redemption—not when God is involved.

Chapter 3

Turning It Around

"So, whether you eat or drink or whatever you do,
do it all for the glory of God."
1 Corinthians 10:31

Knowing God as your Father through faith in Jesus Christ changes everything. It changes how you look at life, how you navigate triumph and disaster, how you make decisions, how you think and speak and work.

It changes how you eat and how you drink. It changes "whatever you do."

And so it changes how you compete.

In his letter to the Ephesians, Paul sums up in typically direct language what our great problem is— the problem that bleeds into all aspects of our sporting lives:

As for you, you were dead in your transgressions and
sins, in which you used to live when you followed the
ways of this world and of the ruler of the kingdom of
the air, the spirit who is now at work in those who are

disobedient. All of us also lived among them at one time, gratifying the cravings of our flesh and following its desires and thoughts. Like the rest, we were by nature deserving of wrath. (Ephesians 2:1-3)

Here is our natural state before God: dead in our sin, following the ways of the world, living for ourselves and therefore deserving of wrath: of eternal separation from God.

Then in verse 4 we read the most marvelous phrase— in fact just a very small but incredible word: "But."

All human history hinges on this word.

But because of his great love for us, God, who is rich in mercy, made us alive with Christ even when we were dead in transgressions—it is by grace you have been saved. And God raised us up with Christ and seated us with him in the heavenly realms in Christ Jesus, in order that in the coming ages he might show the incomparable riches of his grace, expressed in his kindness to us in Christ Jesus.

For it is by grace you have been saved, through faith— and this is not from yourselves, it is the gift of God— not by works, so that no one can boast. For we are God's handiwork, created in Christ Jesus to do good works, which God prepared in advance for us to do.
(v 4-10)

The story the world preaches to us is that we need to prove ourselves, earn our status and perform to certain standards. Every other religion tells this story. The dominant approach to sports is just the same. Work harder, be better and earn success. Then you'll be happy and fulfilled. Then you'll be alive.

The gospel story, however, says that we cannot prove ourselves before God. We cannot earn our salvation. We are "dead in [our] transgressions and sins" (v 1) and we cannot un-kill ourselves. Only God can do that—and in his great mercy, through the work of Jesus, he has. The Christian is freed from the world's story, which tells us that we need to perform to a certain standard to earn love and adulation. We are freed from constantly striving to be respected.

The glory of the gospel is not just that Christians are forgiven but that we have been "raised ... up with Christ and seated ... in the heavenly realms in Christ Jesus" (v 6). When Paul says "in Christ," he's referring to an idea that is central to the New Testament's way of thinking—union with Christ. In fact, this is the most basic definition of a Christian—someone who has been united with Christ by faith.

Have you ever experienced the great joy of seeing your team win the Super Bowl, World Series, or NBA/WNBA Finals? "We won!" you say. But all you did was sit at home on the sofa shouting and eating pizza! Still, there is a sense in which you did win, even though someone else scored the winning goal/touchdown/points.

And now imagine that as you sit on the sofa, your phone rings. It's the captain of your team, inviting you to come and celebrate with the team: to sit on the bus at the victory parade, to hold the trophy and to get the bonus. You still haven't done anything. But you enjoy all the fruits of the victory. "We won!" you shout.

No illustration can do it justice, but in a sense union with Christ is like this. We have won the trophy and we have all the benefits of being the victor, even though we didn't play the game. Our salvation is "not from yourselves, it is the gift of God" (v 8). Because Jesus wins, you win.

When Jesus died, he took our sins with him. They have been dealt with fully and finally. In their place Jesus has given us his perfection, his righteousness. When Jesus rose, we rose with him, and we are now seated with him in heaven. That is how secure our identity is—how secure our salvation is. Now we can call God Father, just as Jesus does. Now we have the Holy Spirit dwelling within us, just as Jesus did. Now we are promised a resurrection from the dead, just as Jesus enjoyed.

If you have faith in Jesus, you did nothing, but you are united to Christ, and you share in all the benefits and joys of his victory. The Victorian-era preacher Charles Spurgeon said:

> *"There is no joy in the world like union with Christ.*
> *The more we can feel it, the happier we are."* [25]

Why did God do all this? To reveal his magnificence: "in order that in the coming ages he might show the incomparable riches of his grace, expressed in his kindness to us in Christ Jesus" (v 7). God's goal for mankind hasn't changed after the fall. He still longs for us to find our joy in him and in doing so to bring him the glory he rightfully deserves. There is no room or need for pride.

Our lives are utterly changed by our union with Christ. It is not just that our salvation for eternity is secured but that our lives today are transformed, as our Father in heaven gives good gifts to his children. Those gifts include "good works, which God prepared in advance for us to do" (v 10). Now, whatever we're doing, we love to do it for the glory of God, delighting in knowing him as our loving Father. Christians are now called to live their lives, as those made in his image, living out our mandate, to rule and reign as God's image-bearers on this earth, doing the "good works prepared in advance" for us.

The theologian (and huge Premier League soccer fan) Dan Strange explains:

> *"Christians are united to Jesus by faith, and we get our old job back. We are restored to our role as rulers over creation, because on our behalf, Jesus did what we couldn't, and now we are 'in him'."* [26]

In the coming chapters we're going to look seriously at how the gospel affects how we play, compete, watch, and engage with our sports, but first let's come back to the four key concepts we've been looking at and see how union with Jesus changes each of these.

Creativity: *In Christ, We Can Now Serve and Worship God in Sports*

In Romans, Paul spends the vast majority of the first eleven chapters explaining how God paid the price for our rebellion through Jesus' life, death and resurrection. In chapter 12 we read how, thanks to "God's mercy," there are wonderful consequences for those who come into a relationship with God through Jesus Christ.

We can now "offer [our] bodies as a living sacrifice, holy and pleasing to God" (v 1). A restored relationship with God means that we have new power to offer our "bodies"—the physical, psychological and spiritual aspects of our lives—to our Creator.

We have a new relationship with the one who gave us our sporting talents to express in the sports community. Paul calls this "true and proper worship." We have been given the capacity to use our sports, once again, to enjoy making his world a better place. Worship is a matter for the whole of our lives, and so, since sports can be an act of worship, we are called not to worship our sports but to worship in our sports. Whether we're scoring a last-second winning three-pointer or missing an open goal, we're called to worship God with every gift, ability and circumstance that he has given us.

New York Yankees pitcher Clay Holmes takes this onto the field and it brings him peace:

> *"You just realize that freedom of when you become that living sacrifice; there's a freedom that comes with it that allows you to just display the talents and the uniqueness that God's given you, and the identity you have in Him, in a way that's much greater than you can do on your own."* [27]

In a similar way Anna Tipton, who competed for Great Britain in the 2012 Paralympics in goalball, understands how her faith helps her think about both her sport and also her disability:

"I feel like goalball is my expression of worship. I'm not a gifted singer. That's never been my thing. But I have got an affinity for playing goalball. And every time I play, it's like my worship to God. If I can do my best on a goalball court, then that's my expression of joy in the way that God has made me. I would never have chosen to have a disability, but actually it's opened up this world to me that I wouldn't have had otherwise." [28]

Community: *In Christ, We Can Love and Serve Others in True Community*

After his last ever tennis match, legendary player Roger Federer expressed admiration for his rival Rafael Nadal:

"I feel extremely grateful. We pushed each other, and together we took tennis to new levels." [29]

This is competition at its finest. Two individuals have strived together to help each other perform with every ounce of their ability. They were able to use their competition to improve, as they used it to increase their awareness of their own strengths and weaknesses, and it led to some of the most remarkable tennis matches in history.

Competition tends to be a way for us to establish our self-worth—we feel better about ourselves when we are better than others. But it does not have to be. If your sense of self is secure because you are united to Christ, it can be used to bring self-knowledge. Theologian Wayne Grudem, writing specifically about competition, outlines this benefit:

"Competition enables each person to find a role in which he or she can make a positive contribution to society and thus a role in which people can work in a way that serves others by doing good for them. Competition is thus a sort of societal functioning of God's attributes of wisdom and kindness, and it is a way society helps people discover God's will for their lives." [30]

Paul himself uses a form of competition as he spurs on the church in Corinth to greater godliness in their use of money when he uses the sacrificial model of the Macedonian churches to urge the Corinthians to do likewise (2 Corinthians 8). Paul, of course, is not calling on the Corinthians to compete in order to be better than the Macedonians but is using their example to inspire the Corinthians to be the best they can be—in this case, by excelling in giving.

The gift of competitive sports is not given for us to puff ourselves up but to make us more like Jesus. He can use the relationships formed in sports and the challenges of success and failure to grow us in godliness. What a kind God we have! He takes what we love and draws us closer to himself through it.

Again, it's worth saying that a Christian's primary community will be their church, not their team. Believers—Jew and Gentile, rich and poor, soccer players and cyclists, elite athletes and club-runners and non-runners—are all part of God's global family, his church (Ephesians 2:11-22). We are all "dearly loved children" (5:1) of our heavenly Father. Our closest relationships as Christians are in the local church.

This is no less true for the professional Christian

athlete whose job makes attendance on a Sunday complicated (just as it does for other shift workers). Elite sports can be desperately lonely, and church may well be the only place where relationships can be formed that are not dependent on performance, money or success.

When Matt Forte played for the Chicago Bears from 2008-2015, he experienced this as he and his wife joined the church she had grown up going to:

> *"When I first starting going, I was Matt Forte, the football player. People recognized me from my career. But now, I am Matt, the Christ-follower who plays football. I'd much rather be more Christian than athlete, and this is how my church family has seen me for the past many years. They know I played and they're aware of all the accomplishments I've achieved on the field, but they see me for my character."* [31]

While it was only once he retired in 2018 and the Fortes moved back to Chicago from New York that he could get as involved in church life as he wanted to, during his pro career Forte still made as much of a priority of church as he could. In Christ, we can enjoy healthy competition and true community in our sports—even as we seek to find community primarily in our church.

Delight: *In Christ, We Can Keep Sports in Their Proper Place, and God Can Use Them to Draw Us Closer to Him*

In the 1990s, Dallas Mavericks scout Donnie Nelson discovered a young German basketballer named Dirk Nowitzki and told his father, Mavericks coach Don, about him. "He was the most unbelievable young player I'd ever seen," Don later remembered.[32] The Mavericks went out of their way to make sure they would be able to draft a player who would eventually become a hall-of-famer. They even hid him in Donnie's basement for the week before the draft. As Nowitzki went on to become an NBA great over 21 years with the Mavericks and lead them to their only NBA championship in 2011, I wonder how often the Nelsons looked back on the time and effort they put into signing him and smiled happily.

Jesus says that discovering the wonder and joy of his kingdom is similar:

> *The kingdom of heaven is like treasure hidden in a field. When a man found it, he hid it again, and then in his joy went and sold all he had and bought that field.*
> *(Matthew 13:44)*

When we find Jesus, we will sell everything for him, and we will do so with joy. As we find our treasure in Jesus alone, we will stop finding it in other things. We will give things up gladly for the kingdom because we know we get far more from Jesus than we could ever be asked to give up for him.

We were made to delight in Jesus alone, and we can do so as we give thanks for his gifts to us. When we know we are loved by our Creator God, and we don't make sports a god, they can be a joy—a gift received with gratitude.

And when it is a gift and not a god, we are able to ride out the inevitable disappointments that come with playing or supporting. Nehemiah told the people of Jerusalem that "the joy of the LORD is your strength" (Nehemiah 8:10). That is, our joy in knowing Jesus is unaffected by our triumphs or sadnesses in any area of life, including the sporting arena. And so if our greatest joy is in knowing him, then we are freed from being puffed up by victory or crushed by defeat or injury.

Adam Pengilly competed in two Winter Olympics for Great Britain in the skeleton, and didn't perform to expectations in either. As he reflects on his career and what he would say to himself as his younger self processed the extreme disappointment, he says:

> "I'd remind him that sport is a real gift. It's a great joy, and it brings real joy and a lot of fun. Although sport can bring joy when you have success, and disappointment when you don't or when you're injured, the thing that brings real joy is knowing the Lord Jesus and having the Creator of the universe adopt you into his family. It is just beyond compare."[33]

Next time you lose—and next time you win—remember: you have the greatest treasure in Christ, and the joy of the Lord is your strength.

Glory: *In Christ, We Can Give God Glory in Sports Through How We Play and What We Say*

We were made to bring God glory in all we do. As the gospel works itself into our hearts, it will transform how we view and compete in our sports. There are three main ways we can bring glory to God in our sports.

1. SATISFIED ATHLETES

We glorify God by finding our total and full satisfaction in him, being grateful for his work in our lives, even when we struggle to understand what he is doing.

This means we will be satisfied in what he is sovereignly doing in our lives: both what we think is good and what we struggle to understand. God is not just glorified when we win or when we're healthy. We can say, with Paul…

> *I eagerly expect and hope that I will in no way be ashamed, but will have sufficient courage so that now as always Christ will be exalted in my body, whether by life or by death. For to me, to live is Christ and to die is gain. (Philippians 1:20-21)*

We have been saved to be able to declare that nothing on this earth is as pleasurable as Christ. We can say that when we die, when we lose all we have—all fame, all wealth and all status—all that we have will be Jesus, and that will be enough. We can say this whether experiencing victory or defeat, or health or injury, for to live is Christ and to die is gain.

We can glorify God as we thank him for what he is doing in us through our sports. Sports are part of how God helps us see that Christ is ultimately what we are to live for.

This is what 400-meter-hurdles Olympic champion and world-record holder Sydney McLaughlin-Levrone came to realize when she came to faith in Christ:

> *"For most of my life, I was driven by fear. Fear of failure, of not living up to people's expectations. I defined myself by my athletic accomplishments.*

Nothing about me mattered if I wasn't winning a race. It wasn't until I suffered crushing defeats on and off the track that I turned to the only One greater than my problems, greater than my fear, and discovered my truest identity, the title that means the most: daughter of God ...

"God [has] delivered me from fear, replacing it with faith. Faith that if I used the gift he'd given me to the best of my ability, win or lose, I would glorify him. In racing and in life, God gives you exactly what you need to run the race he has for you."[34]

2. HUMBLE ATHLETES

In soccer there tends to be two ways of celebrating a goal. In one, you keep others in the background and draw attention to yourself. In the other you share the celebration with the team and make a point of including the player who made the assist.

The Christian will be the second kind of celebrator.

As we recognize our limitations—both morally, in terms of our sinfulness, and practically, in terms of our ability—the right response is to give God all the glory for all our achievements as opposed to pointing towards our work. The gospel is all God's work, and so he rightly deserves all the praise. Our gifts and abilities are all from him, and so again he rightly deserves all the glory. First and foremost, we point upwards to him in our reaction to our achievements and our disappointments. Second, we point to others and celebrate them. Humility, as C.S. Lewis pointed out, is not thinking less of yourself but thinking of yourself less.

3. SERVANT ATHLETES

God's glory is best displayed in Jesus, who "did not come to be served, but to serve" (Mark 10:45). We'll think about this more in chapter 5, but it is worth reflecting on the fact that Jesus is the one we are to imitate as we go about playing or watching sports, no less than in any other area of our lives. We glorify God by not leaving our Christianity in the changing room but letting it transform how we treat others as we play. We are called to serve others as he served. This could be through playing in a position that isn't your best but benefits the team, or going out of your way to care for players struggling to get into the side or recovering from injury, or serving on committees or in sporting governance, aiding others to play the sports you yourself love.

One way this will reveal itself is through us prayerfully serving our friends by sharing Jesus with them (more on this in chapter six). Our job as image-bearers who are united to Christ is to be people who not only live for but shout about the glory and wonder of our Father in heaven.

The Future of Sports

Think back to a moment in your childhood when you were enjoying playing sports. Maybe it was kicking a ball against a wall with your friends, or playing pick-up basketball or a game of flag-football at your local park. Sports were pure and were joyful. You didn't worry massively about winning or losing or about performing to a certain standard. You just played, and it was a delight.

This is how we were made to be.

If you're reading this book, then we imagine that sports are part of who you are. If you know what it is to wake up on your game-day and you can't wait to play because it's the highlight of your week, then you are born to play. You are born to play because you are made in the image of a God who loves to play, and he shows this in how he delighted in creating the world.

C.S. Lewis spoke about how play—whether through reading good books, composing fantastic music or, we would dare to add, playing sports—serves a purpose of acting like a rehearsal for the true playing to come in heaven. The joy of sports is "only the scent of the flower we have not found, the echo of a tune we have not heard, news from a country we have not yet visited."[35]

You can look forward with anticipation to the new creation, where, Zechariah says, "The city streets will be filled with boys and girls playing" (Zechariah 8:5).

This is ultimately what you were made for: to enjoy God for ever. Sports in this time before Jesus' return are a chance to taste and see a glimpse of the future. The great theologian Jonathan Edwards put it better than we ever could:

> "The enjoyment of God is the only happiness with
> which our souls can be satisfied. To go to heaven,
> fully to enjoy God, is infinitely better than the most
> pleasant accommodations here.
>
> "Fathers and mothers, husbands, wives, or children,
> or the company of earthly friends [or the delights of

sports], are but shadows; but God is the substance. These are but scattered beams, but God is the sun. These are but streams. But God is the ocean." [36]

May your enjoyment of your sports on this earth lead you to grow in your excitement about what it will be like to enjoy God, in his new creation, for eternity.

Chapter 4

From Scared to Safe

"I'm seven years old, talking to myself, because I'm scared, and because I'm the only person who listens to me. Under my breath I whisper: Just quit, Andre, just give up. Put down your racket and walk off this court, right now. Go into the house and get something good to eat. Play with Rita, Philly, or Tami. Sit with Mom while she knits or does her jigsaw puzzle. Doesn't that sound nice? Wouldn't that feel like heaven, Andre? To just quit? To never play tennis again? But I can't. Not only would my father chase me around the house with my racket, but something in my gut, some deep unseen muscle, won't let me. I hate tennis, hate it with all my heart, and still, I keep playing, keep hitting all morning, and all afternoon, because I have no choice. No matter how much I want to stop, I don't. I keep begging myself to stop, and I keep playing, and this gap, this contradiction between what I want to do and what I actually do, feels like the core of my life."[37]

Andre Agassi has written one of the most illuminating autobiographies of any athlete. By the age of seven, he associated winning tournaments with safety from the rage and disappointment of his highly driven father, who had told him to use the pain of loss to drive him to success:

> *"You're hurting right now, hurting like heck, but that just means you care. Means you want to win. You can use that. Remember this day. Try to use this day as motivation. If you don't want to feel this hurt again, good, do everything you can to avoid it. Are you ready to do everything? I nod."* [38]

The fear of shame drove him on until he won Wimbledon at the age of 22—and discovered that even winning one of the biggest tournaments in his sport could not heal his wounds and meet the need to find his worth in his performance:

> *"Winning changes nothing. Now that I've won a slam, I know something that very few people on earth are permitted to know. A win doesn't feel as good as a loss feels bad, and the good feeling doesn't last as long as the bad. Not even close."* [39]

Sports are full of wins and losses. More than likely, you will face disappointment more than you will taste success. The question is: how do you feel about yourself in those moments?

An identity which is based on your performance or on your profession will lead to a life of slavery and fear, of doubt and insecurity. Your sports will cease to be something you can delight in and enjoy, and will instead become what it did for Andre—something with which you have at best a love-hate relationship and at worst want to quit but can't, because it fuels your sense of identity.

The Problem: An Achieved Identity

Sports are constantly encouraging us to ask ourselves: am I good enough? If we were to visit living rooms every Saturday or Sunday, we would be struck by how high those who have won are and how low those who have lost feel. For an athlete or a fan, their identity and their sense of worth can be far too wrapped up in their performance and result. Sports psychologists, while taking the view that a strong athletic identity is important to be successful, have also outlined the downsides to that identity—for instance when someone gets injured:

> *"Whether you're elite or lower level, when you're an athlete, sport is such an important part of your identity, so when that is taken away from you when you are injured, it is difficult to handle. You have those feelings of frustration, anger, depression and anxiety—all those things can be common."* [40]

In today's Western culture we tend to look within ourselves to try to find ourselves. Sports appear to offer a very easy way to do this. It seems natural to base our identity on our skills and our successes—to fashion for ourselves an achieved identity. But that is a shaky place in which to find your worth and value.

You'll remember that Eric Liddell's primary emotion as he competed was joy. That was because his sense of self-worth had nothing to do with how fast he ran or where he finished. But for his great rival, Harold Abrahams, as he lined up for his 100m race, fear was the dominant emotion. In the film *Chariots of Fire*, he's depicted as saying, "I will raise my eyes and look down that corridor, four feet wide, with ten lonely seconds to justify my whole existence." *Ten lonely seconds to justify my whole existence.* What a brittle way to view yourself— yet how easily those of us who love sports allow our performance to direct our emotional wellbeing and our sense of ourselves.

The Problem with Losing (and with Winning)

Jonny Wilkinson is one of the most successful rugby union players in history. Having won multiple titles with England in the annual Six Nations international competition, he scored the winning points when England won the World Cup, the pinnacle of the sport, in 2003. And yet, he said...

> *"It feels as if I spent years trying to fight depression with another Six Nations Championship, or some more caps, or titles, or points. 'Surely,' I told myself, 'that will keep you off my back?' It doesn't. It's never enough."* [41]

What's the "it" for you? Making the starting line-up? Setting a new personal record? The team you support winning the championship? Your child being recruited to play in college?

When we base our identity on our performance or that of others, and make it an idol, both winning and losing become issues. As Tim Keller reflects:

"If you make work your identity and you succeed, it'll go to your head. If you fail, it'll go to your heart." [42]

When we lose or face an injury crisis, a Christian athlete who is not living with a secure identity is likely to ask questions of God such as...

- what did I do wrong in my spiritual life which meant God didn't bless me with the win?

- does God not really love me and so allowed me to get injured?

- am I really part of God's team?

And so, in these moments when we need to lean on our relationship with God the most, we often feel too ashamed or angry to go to him.

Winning is no firmer foundation to build our identities on. It also leads to questions around who we are:

- Why does this feeling of joy seem to have gone already?

- Do my friends really care about me or only about the fact that I'm a champion?

- What do I do now that I've achieved all I set out to do at the age of 30?

Jonny Wilkinson and Andre Agassi both made it to the top of their sports. They tasted success and realized that the joy doesn't linger and the problems they felt success would solve ultimately still remain. But what about if you're not like them—you're still chasing your goals, thinking they'll bring uninhibited joy and satisfaction? In some senses, at least those who have had success have been able to see the fallacy of thinking that success will bring happiness. The danger for those of us who are still chasing our goals is that we can go on dreaming that if we could just make that team, hit that time, get that promotion, then we'd feel okay. Wilkinson and Agassi would tell you: you won't. And the Bible tells you: your achievements can never bear the weight of your sense of self-worth.

Only by separating our self-worth from our achievements (or potential ones) can we find satisfaction and security. Ashley Null has worked as a chaplain in five Olympic villages and knows this only too well:

"Only love has the power to make human beings feel truly significant, not achievement. Only knowing that they are loved regardless of their current performance has the power to make Olympians feel emotionally whole." [43]

The Solution: A Received Identity

The Bible describes the new identity we have in Christ in several ways. Union in Christ, as we've seen, is one. But another, and one of the most powerful, is that whereas we were once slaves, now we are "dearly loved children" (Ephesians 5:1):

You are no longer a slave, but God's child; and since
you are his child, God has made you also an heir.
(Galatians 4:7)

There are many ways to live as a slave. A slave to achievement is one. Your happiness and security are based on your success. A slave to approval is another. Your joy is rooted in your approval from others. It is not hard to see how easy it is for athletes (including Christians) to live in this kind of slavery. It's what Harold Abrahams was doing.

And as Christians, we can view our relationship with God primarily as one of slavery. The sporty "religious slave" sees God a bit like an intense coach standing at the finish line of a race with a stopwatch. We're desperate to run quickly to avoid his disappointment. We think that if we don't perform to his standards, he'll shame us or storm off, and we'll have to earn our way back into his good books. Ultimately, we feel afraid of him, and so we act like slaves.

This is not the picture of God that the Bible gives. God is not your a cosmic coach, deciding if you're in or out of his team. He's your heavenly Father, who delights to call you his child. He's not in the stands, sitting back to see how you perform. He's there with you, by his Spirit, in the ups and downs of your sporting life and every other part of your life, helping you every step of the way.

If you are trusting Jesus, then you are no longer a slave but a son or a daughter (Romans 8:15). This is your identity, and it has nothing to do with your sports. Fundamentally, the gospel tells us that we get our identity as a gift, not by trying to be better. Our identity is received, not achieved. We get God as our Father.

And when we say "Father," we don't mean the kind of fathers we too often see in sporting contexts.

Some fathers stand on the sidelines urging their offspring to win by shouting their criticism—needing them to win.

Run faster.

Get the ball.

What are you doing?!

Some fathers care more about how their child makes them look than whether their child is enjoying the game.

Why can't you work harder?

Why can't you play like that other kid?

Some fathers yell and shout and scream, abusing the coach, berating the referee, desperate for victory at all costs.

Ref, that's an awful decision. You're useless!

Coach, put my kid back in! They're better than that other kid.

Some fathers use shame to get their kid to improve.

Use the hurt; let the pain of the loss sink in. Then it can motivate you.

Stop being a wuss—channel the anger; use the crying.

Don't let me down.

God is *not* that kind of father. He is the perfect, true and better Father.

He loves you, and he is with you in all circumstances. He is utterly committed to you, and he's always for you. He knows you'll make mistakes; he knows you'll get it wrong. He chooses to live alongside you every minute of your life and to work with you slowly but surely, through all your vulnerabilities, to make you more and more and more the person he is determined to help you to become.

And none of it depends on your achievements.

> *But God demonstrates his own love for us in this: while we were still sinners, Christ died for us. (Romans 5:8)*

God shows his love for us in the most incredible way: it is shocking; it is extreme. In Jesus, God himself hung on a cross. Life itself was put to death. For you. Why?

Because of all your good deeds? Your moral perfection?

Because of your achievements in life?

Because of your performance on an athletic field?

No. It was before any of that. Jesus died for you as a sinner. All you brought was your sin. You offered him nothing. Yet even so, you are loved:

Not because your talent.

Not because of your performance.

Not because of your fame.

Not because of your success.

But because of the God who is love, for his love never fails. He loves you because he loves you. Your identity as his child is something you can only receive from him, not achieve for yourself.

And this changes how we compete.

1. We Can Compete Feeling Safe and Joyful

"Those same thousands of opportunities to feel shame in sport also give God countless moments to speak to his children, to push back the darkness from around them, to root his promises in their hearts while in the heat of battle, to be at work in them so that they lean more into their calling, competing with an ever increasing sense of God's eternal assurance of his love and their worth." [44]

If we are secure in our identity, we can reflect safely on both the highs and lows of our sports. When we trust that God, as our Father, is working positively in our lives and know that God, as our Father, loves us unconditionally, then we can deal with anything our sports throw at us, including failure, injury, getting cut, and retirement.

Nick Foles famously led the Philadelphia Eagles to win the Super Bowl in 2017, having replaced their regular quarterback when he was injured. He had spent most of his career as a backup, and by 2021 he was the Chicago Bears' third-choice quarterback and considering his future. You would imagine such a player would be full of doubts, insecurities, bitterness or self-recrimination. But Foles knew his identity was a gift:

"It doesn't matter if you're the first string, second string, third string; you've got to know who you are as a human being and what your identity is ... It can't be in this game. It's got to be in something greater, and I've always said mine's in Jesus Christ.

*I was a third-string quarterback tonight. I was just
a third string—that's my label. But at the end of the
day, that's not who I am."* [45]

God wants us to know our received identity and feel safe
and secure in it. His Spirit works day by day to remind
us of our adoption into his family:

*The Spirit you received does not make you slaves,
so that you live in fear again; rather, the Spirit you
received brought about your adoption to sonship. And
by him we cry, "Abba, Father." The Spirit himself
testifies with our spirit that we are God's children.*
(Romans 8:15-16)

This means we can be joyful and grateful as we play.
Australian Olympic high jumper Nicola McDermott
(now Nicola Olyslagers) is well known for competing
with a smile, whether she clears the bar or not. She is
clear about what brings the smile to her face:

*"When your identity is based on what you do—a
performance-based identity—it will never satisfy.
I found that I could never jump high enough to be
truly satisfied. But when your identity is based on the
fact that you are loved by God... That allows me to
perform out of joy and freedom."* [46]

If you see everything as a gift from God, then your
response to the abilities he has given you and the
opportunities he has provided is to receive them with
joy and thanksgiving.

The trainer who massages you after a race or match...
The fan or family member who shouts encouragement...

The coach who works hard to help you improve... All of these are given by God, to bless us. We live in a world where God is totally in control and always acting as our loving Father.

Why don't you stop now, think back over your sporting efforts this last week, and give thanks for some specific things God has given to you?

2. We Can Deal With the Pain Sports Bring Us

Sports are filled with far more disappointment than success. At every Olympic Games only a tiny percentage of the athletes win (not to mention the hundreds who didn't even make it through their national trials). In every professional and amateur team-sport season, only one team lifts the trophy. And virtually every athlete will experience injury or failing to make the team at some point.

If you live as a child of God, it transforms your perspective on the disappointments because with God nothing is wasted. The writer to the Hebrews helps us understand what God is doing in these moments:

My son, do not make light of the Lord's discipline,
and do not lose heart when he rebukes you,
because the Lord disciplines the one he loves,
and he chastens everyone he accepts as his son.

Endure hardship as discipline; God is treating you as his children. For what children are not disciplined by their father? If you are not disciplined—and everyone undergoes discipline—then you are not legitimate, not true sons and daughters at all. (Hebrews 12:5-8)

Difficulties in our lives and in our sports are not a sign of God's displeasure with us but instead a mark of his love: "the Lord disciplines *the ones he loves*." He may not do what we would like or give us what we were hoping for. He may take away things that we love. But the one who sent his Son to the cross for us is always working for us because he loves us. When we look at the cross, we are able to say that...

we know that in all things God works for the good of those who love him, who have been called according to his purpose. (Romans 8:28)

God works all things, even the painful ones, for our good. This does not mean that all circumstances are in themselves good. There is much that is wrong in our world that we need to acknowledge as such. Even injury is a result of the fall—a sign of our broken world. But injuries can remind us that our identity is received from him, not found in our athletic ability, and can help us long for the world to come, where there will be no more sickness and crying and pain. We don't need to pretend that bad things are good things; we do need to trust that God will use them for our good.

But what is the good that God is doing?

For those God foreknew he also predestined to be conformed to the image of his Son, that he might be the firstborn among many brothers and sisters. (v 29)

Through all things, even the hardest things in life, God is making us more like Jesus. This is a wonderful thing. Jesus was courageous, compassionate, wise, thoughtful, joyful and full of love. There is not a better person who ever walked the earth. Being more like him is a better goal than any championship or medal or PR. While it may be hard for a naturally competitive athlete to read, God's primary desire for you is that you keep trusting Christ and becoming more like him. He desires this for you far more than he wants you to win a trophy or achieve all your goals—and that is a good thing. His ultimate goal for you is to be like his magnificent Son, showing others around you how great it is to know him and one day enjoying life with him for ever. Perhaps we need to pray that this becomes our ultimate desire for ourselves too. When our greatest ambitions are athletic ones, the problem is not that our dreams are too big but that they're too small.

Look at My Boy

Andre Agassi felt his father never truly loved him. His worth was entirely dependent on his performance.

The Olympic swimmer Chad Le Clos never needed to feel like that. In 2012 an interview with his dad went viral around the world as he yelled delightedly into the camera, "Look at my boy! He's so beautiful."

This is how your heavenly Father views you in Christ. You have nothing to prove to him. His love is the "it" you need. He is the one who gives meaning to your existence. No sporting success of yours will increase his delight in you, and no failure will dampen it. Remember that today—and on the next game day!

Chapter 5

From Self-Focused to Serving

With four laps to go in her 5,000m 2016 Olympic qualifying heat in Rio, American runner Abbey D'Agostino was in with a chance of qualifying for the final when she was tripped. She could have kept running. Her coach had told her before the race that if she fell over, just to dust herself off and get back in the race. There was about a mile to go. There was time to catch up.

Instead, she turned around to New Zealander Nikki Hamblin, whose fall had inadvertently tripped D'Agostino. She helped Hamblin up and encouraged her to finish the race.

What prompted D'Agostino to stop and help a fellow competitor in that moment? What caused her to be willing to care for another at the expense of her own hopes on the highest stage?

"Although my actions were instinctual at that moment, the only way I can and have rationalized it is that God

prepared my heart to respond that way ... This whole time here he's made clear to me that my experience in Rio was going to be about more than my race performance—and as soon as Nikki got up, I knew that was it." [47]

Every Christian plays sports for more than just their performance, as we saw in the last chapter. And that will change how we behave in our teams and races—in how we think of and treat those around us.

Changed Lives Come from a Changed Identity

As God's children, we are called "to work out [our] salvation with fear and trembling, for it is God who works in [us] to will and to act in order to fulfill his good purpose" (Philippians 2:12-13). We don't work *for* our salvation (that's a gift from God, in Christ). We do work *out* our salvation—we live it out in each area of our lives. And we do this with the confidence that God is the one already at work in us, helping us to live out his plans for us. We are completely saved, but we are not finished works. So we are to "continue to work out [our] salvation"—in an ongoing process of becoming more and more like Jesus.

Someone once asked the great sculptor Michelangelo how he approached a large chunk of marble as he went about turning it into an intricate work of art. He described his work as "liberating an angel from the stone." Sports coaching expert Timothy Gallwey described coaching in similar terms: "Coaching is unlocking a person's potential to maximize their own performance." [48] This is what God is doing in your life, shaping and molding you more and more into his likeness and helping us "fulfill his good purpose" in our lives. He gives us all we need to do this.

As we've seen, we are being restored back into the original image we were created to be—conformed into the image of Jesus, the perfect human. So, it makes sense to look at Jesus! We ponder him. We dwell on him and his life and his character. We seek to "have the same mindset as Christ Jesus" (v 5). And Paul spells out what that looks like:

> *If you have any encouragement from being united with Christ ... do nothing out of selfish ambition or vain conceit. Rather, in humility value others above yourselves, not looking to your own interests but each of you to the interests of the others ... Have the same mindset as Christ Jesus. (v 1-4)*

Because we know that we are united with Christ, and therefore know that we are securely loved, we can—and will—value others above ourselves, prioritizing their interests over our own.

And that will make us very different in our approach to sports.

Imitating Christ in our Sports

It's not uncommon to hear a athlete say that in order to be successful, they have to be selfish. One of the most famous of all, Michael Jordan, literally said just that:

> *"To be successful you have to be selfish or else you never achieve."* [49]

A probably apocryphal story recounts Jordan's coach once telling him that he was being selfish. "There's no I in team," he said, to which Jordan replied, "But there is a me!" Tim Noakes, a runner and sports psychologist, has written about "selfish athlete syndrome," where he makes the same point—that to be truly successful the athlete has to think about himself more than others, especially in his family commitments.

Athletes often make sacrifices to succeed. But often, the one who bears the sacrifice is not the athlete involved. It might be your family losing out on time with you or a spouse having to plan things round your sporting commitments; it might be an opponent being mistreated; it might be a teammate left waiting for a pass.

As Ashley Null diagnoses:

> *"Non-Christian athletes are able to show incredible commitment to their sports and make the tremendous sacrifices that are required. But the source of this power is selfish ambition rooted in a spiritual insecurity that constantly drives them to prove their worth. And the difficulties they experience in their private lives testify only too well to the destructive consequences of the power that they have given themselves over to in order to win."* [50]

Let's be honest—Christian athletes are often tempted to put themselves first too.

But now reread Paul's words to the Philippians:

> *Therefore if you have any encouragement from being united with Christ, if any comfort from his love, if any common sharing in the Spirit, if any tenderness*

and compassion, then make my joy complete by being like-minded, having the same love, being one in spirit and of one mind. Do nothing out of selfish ambition or vain conceit. Rather, in humility value others above yourselves, not looking to your own interests but each of you to the interests of the others.

In your relationships with one another, have the same mindset as Christ Jesus:

who, being in very nature God,
    did not consider equality with God something to be
    used to his own advantage;
rather, he made himself nothing
    by taking the very nature of a servant,
    being made in human likeness.
And being found in appearance as a man,
    he humbled himself
    by becoming obedient to death—
        even death on a cross! (2:1-8)

Christians have a new priority and a new power to live by. We are not called to live like Michael Jordan but like Jesus (who, by the way, by any secular definition, did not have a successful life). Jesus was God himself, yet he had a humble and tender heart. This is a dramatic challenge to the "me, me, me" self-focus that often dominates the world of sports.

We can sum up Jesus' mindset—the one that we're called to imitate—as *What is good for other people?* That was what ultimately led to him coming to earth and dying in our place on the cross. He went from being eternally worshiped in an eternal paradise where there was no suffering or pain or death to coming to this earth, experiencing pain and tiredness and suffering for the first time. He was willing to be flogged, spat on and beaten, and suffered the ultimate pain and humiliation of crucifixion and separation from the eternal relationship of love he had with the Father. Why did he do this? Because he was willing to serve. Because he asked, *What is good for other people?*

Our perspective on our sporting lives will be challenged by simply asking that question. But as we ask it, we will find we have so many opportunities to live like Jesus— to "shine among [people in the world] like stars in the sky" (v 15).

This is what John did. John was in his first year at college in the UK, and was desperate to play in the soccer team. He didn't make the team but was still committed to training. He was the first one there and the last one to leave. Still he wasn't picked. Then, halfway through the season, as injuries hit, he was called up for his first game. He was delighted and told all his friends and family.

The match was away from home, and they took a bus to the game. On the way, the bus got caught in heavy traffic. They were cutting it fine for kick-off and so the captain told his team to get changed on the bus. It was only then that the captain realized he'd forgotten his boots. He looked numerous times in his bag, on the floor of the bus, anywhere he could think of—but they weren't there. He had no boots. He could not play.

John didn't hesitate: "Mate, you're the same size as me. Take mine."

The captain was gobsmacked. "But what are you going to do?"

"It's okay. I'll go on the bench," John replied. "It's more important that you play than me—so take my boots."

So the captain did. But at half-time, he stopped his team talk and started to interrogate John. He simply couldn't understand why he would give him his boots.

"We all know how much you want to play in this team. We know how long you've waited for this opportunity and how hard you've trained, and yet now you've given me your boots. What are you doing?"

After the game, on the bus on the way back, the captain sat next to John and again asked him what had motivated him to act in the way that he did. For two hours, John shared his faith in Jesus with him. Six weeks later the captain came to an event at his church. Three months later he put his trust in Jesus. All because one guy in the squad had quietly valued others above himself, had asked "What is good for other people?" and had sacrificially given up his boots.

What might that look like for you? How can you adopt the same mindset as Jesus in the way you support, train and play?

How Can I Serve in my Sports?
SEEK JOY

Paul starts to answer the question of what it looks like to "work out your salvation" (Philippians 2:12) by saying:

Do everything without grumbling or arguing, so that you may become blameless and pure, "children of God

without fault in a warped and crooked generation."
Then you will shine among them like stars in the sky
as you hold firmly to the word of life. And then I will
be able to boast on the day of Christ that I did not run
or labor in vain. But even if I am being poured out like
a drink offering on the sacrifice and service coming
from your faith, I am glad and rejoice with all of you.
(Philippians 2:14-17)

Paul is primarily speaking about relationships within the church and among other Christians, but this flows out into our life in the world. No grumbling or arguing. Instead, a joy in others' gain, even when we are facing hardships ourselves.

Anyone who has been in a sports team knows how easy it is to complain. We grumble about our teammates and coaches, either directly to them or more likely behind their backs:

She shouldn't be training with us!

If I was in charge, they wouldn't play in that position.

We love to grumble about and to opponents:

Why did you do that?

That team are always so arrogant. I'm glad we're not like them.

We love to grumble about officials and referees:

How on earth could they get such a simple decision wrong?

They always penalize us more than the opposition!

Sports are full of complaining. How radical and distinctive would it be to be known for contentment and joy?! To be known as someone who is quicker to hold their own hand up than blame others—as someone who is known for building others up and erring on the side of kindness rather than criticism.

Of course there are times when it is right to raise injustices with the right people. This is not a command to accept abuse, bullying or injustice. But it is a reminder that asking yourself what is good for other people will look like less grumbling and more kindness. A "you first" attitude is one that leads to joy, and it's an attitude that the Christian is not permitted to leave at home or in the changing room (nor should we want to). Work to see and celebrate the good in others. Look to Christ and seek, with his help, to adopt his attitude.

SERVE OTHERS ON THE FIELD

What does valuing others above yourself look like in sports? It looks like loving our teammates and our opponents.

First, we love our teammates by remembering that whether we win doesn't matter as much as how we play.

Paul was already a professional soccer player when he became a Christian. His new identity changed his view of others:

> *"My whole life changed; it's a life-changing thing [becoming a Christian]. There was something more important than soccer, although soccer remained very important ... I would think of my teammates more as people and less as just a good player. So,*

I'd be more interested in that side. I'd want to be a good ambassador for God. I was aware of that all the time."

Thinking of our teammates as people, and loving them as people, is what it means to love them well.

Second, we play our best. Just because we recognize that winning isn't everything, it doesn't mean we need to lose a competitive edge. This means a full commitment, even if we're playing rec sports and just turning up to train once a week and play at the weekend. We love our team by giving our all when we are there, striving hard to win. The rules of the game have been set, and as long as we compete within them we have an obligation, out of love to both our teammates and the opposition, to compete as hard as we can.

Val Gin, an accomplished scholar and college volleyball coach, reflected on this in her coaching of Christian athletes:

"As a Christian, you can recognize the interaction that you have with a competitor or a teammate as a God moment: that you're the presence of Christ to your opponent on the team. So to do that you're going to play your darnedest, your hardest, so that you can bring out the best in your opponent and in your teammate." [51]

This is Christian competitiveness.

Third, we play fair. Doing what's right is more important to us than doing what's necessary to win. Russell Henley was a pro golfer who started taking his faith seriously in 2019. In 2019, he was playing a Tour event in Mexico and had just shot a second-round 69 when he realized he had ended his round with a ball that was not his, which is against Tour rules. No one else knew. It had not benefited him. He could have got away with it.

Henley called a penalty on himself. He went from making the cut and picking up a good check to heading home.

I'm a Christian," Henley said afterwards. "The Lord has opened my eyes to the truth. There are going to be trials in a person's life, for all of us."[52]

It is not only our relationship with the rules but with opponents that our faith will inform. If we see our opponent not as our enemy but as our neighbor, and moreover a neighbor whom Jesus tells us to love as ourselves, it transforms our attitude towards them. We treat our opponent in the way we want to be treated: with respect. We want a fair game. We want a good contest. We want our opponent to push us to perform at our best. People often think that being loving and being competitive is an "either or" but in this setting, love is to be competitive!

Pause right now and think about how you have been treating opponents both during and after matches or competitions. Think about what you say when you've won or lost. Think about how honest you are in your play. Think about the way you speak about the opposition when only your teammates are in earshot.

What will it look like to "work out your salvation" in this area?

LOVE PEOPLE OFF THE FIELD

There are two dangers for Christians when we think about life off the field in the world of sports.

The first mistake is to be someone who is there but never shares: someone who spends plenty of time with their team but hides their faith and doesn't live in a distinctive way. We'll think more about this in the next chapter.

But the second mistake is to share but never be there: someone who is willing to speak of their faith but is not really involved in people's lives in any meaningful way. In 1 Thessalonians 2:7-8, Paul speaks of how he loved some new and some not-quite-yet Christians in Thessalonica "so much [that] we were delighted to share with you not only the gospel of God but our lives as well." He was willing to share both his life and the gospel with them. He was there, and he shared! Developing real, lasting friendships will involve commitment, sacrifice and vulnerability. "Being there" will involve being involved in our friends' lives so we know not just how they are performing in their sport but how they are doing in their wider lives.

We can do this by being committed to turning up to a decent number of social events, deliberately seeking time to speak with others and being intentional in asking questions which point beyond sports. Just a simple "How is life at home at the moment?" can be a good way to deepen friendship beyond the surface level. It's as we get to know our teammates as people that we will be able, sensitively and wisely, to bring Jesus into our friends' lives as we laugh and cry with them—as we walk together through life. And we have to be there in order to do that.

It is not easy to do this wisely. While there are so many great things about being immersed in a sports team, there are also always temptations to live like the world and not like Jesus.

We are called to be different amid the culture of a changing room which misuses alcohol, and sex and which is full of coarse language; amid gossip on the bus to the game; amid heckling and abuse on the terraces. It isn't legalistic to say that a Christian's life must change. Imagine being called up to play for your country—you wouldn't turn up in your unwashed team jersey anymore. No, you would put on the brand new national jersey that had been given to you. Who you are affects what you put on and how you play. The New Testament tells us, as "dearly loved children" to "clothe yourselves with the Lord Jesus Christ" (Colossians 3:12; Romans 13:14). We are called to be there *and* to look like Jesus. And as with every other aspect of our sporting lives as God's children, the key to doing so is to remember who we are.

As we close this chapter, it is well worth stopping and reflecting. Have a read through Ephesians 5:1-20, and as you do so think about your own sporting context and particularly the opportunities you have to love and serve others in a Christlike way off the field when traveling or socializing. What will it look like for you to "follow God's example" (v 1) in...

- your purity (v 3)?

- your speech (v 4-6)?

- your relationship with alcohol (v 18)?

Remember, you are in your team, on and off the field, to serve others, not yourself. You'll remember that, and you'll be pleased to live like that, to the extent that you keep remembering that your brother Jesus is the one who "did not come to be served, but to serve, and to give his life as a ransom for many" (Mark 10:45).

What will change as you head to your next game or practice asking yourself, "What is good for other people?"

Chapter 6

Pray, Play, Say

His name was Gwyon, and he was the school cricket captain. The school's starting lineup was short of a few senior players and they needed some younger ones to fill in—so I (Graham) was picked. Our opponents were about 50 miles away, just outside Cardiff, the capital city of Wales.

We beat them soundly, and as I got onto the bus to head home, the only spare seat was next to Gwyon. It was a long journey, and we hardly knew each other. Having finished talking about the match, I asked him whether he was going to play cricket on the Saturday, and then I asked him what he would do with his Sunday. To my utter surprise, he told me he'd go to church.

My brain was scrambled. "Does your mother still make you go to Sunday School at the age of 18?!" I asked.

Instead of batting back my inappropriate question, Gwyon answered graciously and calmly. He said he chose to go to church because he was a Christian. We talked a bit more, and after that, all I remember thinking was how on earth this normal guy, a good athlete who could have a laugh, could possibly be a Christian.

This was the beginning of my seven-year journey to me putting my faith in Jesus. Meeting this normal, gentle and gracious athlete was the start of it.

My story is the story of what happens when a Christian athlete grasps their identity, lets it transform how they live and then takes the opportunity to speak of Jesus to their friends.[53] Before this conversation, I had already developed great respect for two boys in my own year at school, Geraint and John, both of whom were excellent cricketers and known as Christians. Yet it was on this particular journey home from a game, sitting next to Gwyon, that I first felt a significant challenge about my complacency towards God.

Later, Gwyon would tell me how he'd been challenged at church the day before to share something of his faith. He hadn't done so before and was scared. I'm so grateful that he didn't let feeling afraid stop him from speaking about Jesus with me on that minibus trip home.

During that journey, Gwyon was playing his part in living out Jesus' final command to his disciples, sometimes known as the Great Commission:

> *All authority in heaven and on earth has been given to me. Therefore go and make disciples of all nations, baptizing them in the name of the Father and of the Son and of the Holy Spirit, and teaching them to obey everything I have commanded you. And surely I am with you always, to the very end of the age.*
>
> *(Matthew 28:18-20)*

That command was not just for those who were with him at the time but for all Christians. Gwyon heard that call, and the rest, as they say, is history.

Jesus' followers are called to go to share his gospel with "all nations," from every corner of the globe. The word used here is *ethne*, which means "people groups" or "cultures." In a sense, and without wishing to push it too far, you can see your sporting network as a people group: a group of interlinked humans with one area of belonging in common—your sport. There are fewer bigger groups of people with a common interest in the world than the "sports community." It cuts across racial, religious and ethnic backgrounds. Nelson Mandela, who opposed racist apartheid policies in South Africa and then became the first President of the country after apartheid had been defeated, even once said:

"Sport has the power to change the world. It has the power to inspire. It has the power to unite people in a way that little else does. It speaks to youth in a language they understand. Sport can create hope where once there was only despair. It is more powerful than governments in breaking down racial barriers. It laughs in the face of all types of discrimination." [54]

The call from Jesus to make disciples of all people groups undoubtedly applies, then, to making disciples in the world of sports. That is a daunting instruction, but Jesus also gives us the comfort of the reminder that he oversees everything and the promise that he will be with us everywhere we go.

Will you be one of those who will go and seek to make disciples in the world of sports? Will you respond to Jesus' challenge and look to make him known in your sports team?

But *how*? We're going to look at a few verses from the end of Paul's letter to the Colossians which contain clear instructions about how we can effectively share the gospel. Of course, these verses are not specifically about sporting contexts. They can be applied to our workplaces and neighborhoods just as much as locker rooms, football fields, and gyms. But wherever we are and whoever we're with, Paul's encouragement to us is to *pray, play* and *say, together*.

Pray

We've seen that the first core building block we need to understand is our new received identity in Jesus. We are now children with a heavenly Father, eternally secure. We pray to "our Father in heaven" (Matthew 6:9)—not as an act of performance but in utter dependence. We pray knowing that our Father is in total control, ruling and reigning in heaven.

Sharing our faith begins with praying to our Father. "Devote yourselves to prayer, being watchful and thankful," says Paul (Colossians 4:2). Athletes know all about dedication and devotion. At the heart of our evangelism is full devotion to prayer and a persistence in it. Perhaps the Colossian church had grown prayerless and lacking in zeal, and Paul was calling them to return to devoted prayer. Perhaps you need to hear that call too.

Paul wants the Colossians' prayers to be marked by thanksgiving. As the pastor Dick Lucas says, "Prayer can no more exist without praise than true praise without prayer: the one fuels the other."[55] It is out of an overflow from our joy in the gospel that we will share our faith with those in our sports teams. Having started with praise, Paul asks these Christians to...

> *pray for us, too, that God may open a door for our message, so that we may proclaim the mystery of Christ, for which I am in chains. Pray that I may proclaim it clearly, as I should. (v 3-4)*

Amazingly, Paul doesn't ask for prayer that the doors of the prison he is writing from will open; he asks for the Colossians to pray that more doors for the gospel will be opened. We too can pray for those who preach the gospel and to whom we can invite our friends to come and hear about Jesus and ask their questions. But we can also be those who proclaim Christ; so Paul is encouraging us to pray for ourselves—that God would give us chances to share about Jesus.

Prayer does work. That's Katy's story. She went to college and was very focused on her sport. She met some fantastic girls on the team, and they became some of her closest friends while in college. Some of them were Christians. Katy had never met "sporty" Christians before, so she was quite intrigued by them and found them really interesting to talk to. She began to have really great conversations with one of them in particular. Katy began going to church. Eventually, she found herself sitting in a prayer meeting where

Christian athletes met to pray that their friends would come to faith. It was here that she discovered that her friend had been praying for her and six of her netball friends to become Christians.

Not only was that prayer soon answered, but Katy went on to play for her college team for three more years and became a bold witness herself, seeing many others follow Jesus during her time on the team.

Who are you going to start praying for?

Play

Be wise in the way you act toward outsiders; make the most of every opportunity. (v 5)

Whether watching in the stands, traveling on the team bus or grabbing a bite to eat after training, the call remains: live wisely, actively looking for opportunities to show the difference Jesus makes. It is through our conduct that questions will be provoked. Just like the story of John who gave up his soccer boots, our attitude and actions in our sports can encourage people to inquire more about our faith.

The Australian evangelist Sam Chan, in his book *How to Talk about Jesus (Without Being That Guy)*, talks about the importance of three things in our evangelism:

- Our logos: what I say

- Our pathos: the way I make you feel

- Our ethos: how I live

He notes:

"The ethos plays a disproportionately large part in personal evangelism. What we say is important. But the more closely someone knows us, the more they will be persuaded by our way of life rather than merely by what we say." [56]

As we saw in the last chapter, Paul loved the Thessalonians so much that he was sharing his life with them. Are we willing to do the same with our sports friends? This will be costly, in terms of both our time and our money, but it is worth it.

How we live on and off the field matters. We can seek wisdom from God's word and in prayer and also from others in our churches about how to approach various situations. Still, we won't always get this right—but that itself can lead to important gospel conversations as we recognize mistakes we have made and own up to them in front of our friends.

Sarah was a soccer player who noticed a difference in how her Christian friend Priscilla acted:

"We used to walk to training together, and she started telling me about how she went to church. I wasn't really interested at first, but as I got to know her a bit more, I started to wonder what it was all about and why she was going to church. She stood out to me as being different because there was something special in her—a different quality about her. She was so full of life and an amazing friend—so loving and caring— and I wanted to find out why she was like this.

*"One night I got back from a soccer social, and I
don't really know what drove me to send the text,
but I asked Priscilla if I could go to church with her
tomorrow. We began to then read the Bible together,
and in time I put my trust in Jesus."* [57]

There is no reason why you can't be a "Priscilla" in your
own sporting situation.

So we pray to our Father, we play differently because
we're his children—and then we need to say something
about his Son.

Say

*Let your conversation be always full of grace, seasoned
with salt, so that you may know how to answer
everyone. (v 6)*

Part of the reason you have been gifted and are passionate
for sports is so that you would be able to speak to those
you are competing with. You have a wonderful message
to share, which your friends need to hear. And as you
remember who you are, you can have courage and take
risks to go and share Jesus. Dan Strange encourages us
in *Making Faith Magnetic*, his book that helps us speak
into the big questions our friends have:

*"We are small, often tired, dispirited, and seemingly
defeated, but our identity is stable and secure. And
when we remember that, we can proclaim with
increasing confidence to the scared shaky-selves
all around us the magnetically attractive hope and
certainty that the Lord of history offers."* [58]

Our aim is to offer people the same joy for which we ourselves are thankful—Jesus. This is the grace we offer. He is what makes our conversation "taste" different. Make sure you are enjoying Jesus and taking time to think about how wonderful he is and how much he has done and is doing for you—that will help you want to share about him. It's hard to make your speech full of him if you haven't been enjoying the taste of the gospel yourself.

Our speech can even be full of flavor when that flavor is less sweet and more spicy. God can use our brokenness and mistakes as well as our strength and godliness to draw others to himself. Anastasia Chitty was on the Great Britain Olympic rowing program during an especially challenging season. She recounts how it was during her suffering and failures that she was able to speak of grace:

> "It was such a hard environment; I was always tired, and I was also so aware of my sin—I could get quite nasty and upset people within the team. And yet, the Lord still used that. I wasn't witnessing because people saw something of Christ in me, sadly. I was more witnessing when I could share that Christ was the answer to my brokenness. That could be painful at times, but it did give me opportunities. As a Christian, I could acknowledge my sin and my brokenness and the hurt that it could cause at times. And yet I [could share that in Jesus I] have forgiveness, and so can others."[59]

As we share life with others, through both joy and pain, it will lead to questions which we are called to be prepared to answer, making the most of every opportunity. It is God alone who can open people's eyes to trust and enjoy him themselves, but it is our job to go and point them to the one in whom life is truly found.

Gwyon Jenkins did just that. He responded to the challenge he had heard in church; he lived differently to those around him and was willing to make the most of the opportunity that presented itself when a new member of his team asked him what he did on Sundays. It was as simple as that.

Will you do the same in your sporting context and actively seek to say something of your Lord and Saviour to those around you?

Together

Colossians 4:2-6 is not quite the end of Paul's letter to this church. In the last few verses of Colossians, he turns to list some of those who are involved in his ministry, and to thank them. It's a great reminder that there is teamwork involved in the call to share the gospel. You may be the only Christian in your sporting context, and it is good to pray that God would bring a fellow believer or two into the team. But remember that you already have a team behind you. It's your church. They can pray for you, encourage you… and help you.

Sam Chan talks about how important it is for our friends to meet other Christians:

> *"Typically, when we as Christians get fired up to do evangelism, we go out solo. These solo efforts are admirable and worthy. But the result is that we are*

*the one and only bozo in the room who believes in
the Jesus story. And no matter how true the story
is, no matter how much evidence we can produce, no
matter how logically we argue, our story—as true,
logical, and rational as it is—remains unbelievable
because there's no other person in the room who also
believes it.*"[60]

So, seek to (as Chan puts it) "merge your universes" so
your non-Christian friends can meet your Christian
ones. Think deliberately about how you can get people
from both your church and your sports team together
so they can meet each other.

An avid distance runner, Gill Bland, explains how this
has worked for her in her church:

*"As I've tapped into the burgeoning London distance
running scene over time, I've started to wonder how
my faith and sport work together. Now, a few times
a year, we meet after work at church and go for a
40-minute run around the capital before returning
to munch on pizza and hear a brief interview with
a Christian runner. So far, I've been able to invite
seven of my competitor friends along, and I've also
had the benefit of sharing my love of running with my
church family. These events have pushed me to make
the effort to invite people and have given me a way
to start sharing my faith more clearly. They've also
helped with opening the door to talk about some of
the harder topics like sin.*"[61]

There are thousands of other stories like this, as people
have seen the benefit in inviting friends to various

events and to their church services where the gospel will be proclaimed.

How can you invite your church friends to help you share Christ with your sporting friends?

God Is at Work

A mistake many of us often make is to read stories about people like Gwyon, Priscilla and Gill and think, "I could never do that... That would never happen to me... My friends just aren't like that..."

Perhaps you could never do it—but God's Spirit lives in you to enable you to do things you can't do alone. And it is God who works through his gospel to win people's hearts—not you. So, unless God has given up reaching people (and he hasn't), it could happen. Your friends may not seem interested—so pray for them. I wasn't interested either—until Gwyon opened his mouth.

As we pray, play and say, God works. He really does. Let's close with the story of two professional soccer players coming to faith simply because someone was praying, playing, and saying.

First, Wayne Jacobs was an experienced professional at Bradford City and a follower of Jesus. He used to carpool with a young defender called Darren Moore. He used those opportunities to share Jesus with him. Later, Darren, having eventually come to faith, said that "I knew about the Lord, but what I believed was that playing soccer and serving the Lord was impossible to do." Through his conduct and his speech, Wayne showed Darren that in fact it was possible, and Darren put his trust in Jesus.

After a few years of being discipled by Wayne, Darren moved to Portsmouth Football Club, an EPL team. There he met Linvoy Primus, who had arrived initially on a week-long trial and impressed the manager, Harry Redknapp, enough to earn a contract. He began to room with Darren on away trips. As Darren chatted with him, he discovered that Linvoy had begun to explore Christianity after his wife came to faith. So Darren invited him to a Bible study at the club. There were several Christians in the team (Harry Redknapp, not a believer himself, has spoken of how the equipment room was turned into a prayer room!) and meeting with them made Christianity plausible for Linvoy.

Linvoy was an unlikely convert, just as the apostle Paul himself was. How did Paul know the gospel could work in anyone's life? Because it had worked in his, even when he had been fully committed to defying and defeating Christ and his people. Linvoy realized the same thing and now spends his time looking to share the good news of Jesus with everyone he meets.

So you may know people who you think would never come to Christ: the foul-mouthed coach, or the promiscuous teammate who always finds him or herself with someone different on a night out, or the friend who you've shared the gospel with many times with no obvious engagement. Nobody is beyond hope—nobody. Maybe the way the Lord will provide another Christian in your team is through saving one of your friends.

Jesus is risen, he has all authority, and he is with us. He commands us to go and share him—to pray, to play, and to say. Let's go!

Chapter 7

A Word for...
Fans

Every week, the highest-rated television programs are usually live NFL games. Every year, millions of us will go to a college or NFL stadium—many of us multiple times. And that's just football. Other sports have equally passionate fan-bases.

Even those who have little interest in sports most of the time become fans when major events come around. When the Olympic Games and soccer World Cups or European Championships roll around, they become the most watched television broadcasts of the year—and when it comes to the Olympics, for a couple of weeks we develop strange obsessions and become armchair experts in gymnastics, diving, or boccia.

But what does it look like to be a fan who also follows Jesus? How does being a disciple shape how we support our team or country (or new-found Olympic taekwondo hero)?

Many of us may have never really thought about this question. Or maybe we've thought about it and decided that it's too hard to work out. Or perhaps we subconsciously (or deliberately) choose to leave our allegiance to Christ at the turnstiles as we go to support our team. So as you read, get your particular sports team or passion fixed in your mind and analyze how you view and approach your support of it.

Come with us and answer the question: if you're a Christian, is there a distinctive way to be a fan?

The Joy

Why does watching sports engage us so much?

Sports encapsulate the full kaleidoscope of human emotions, all packaged in a few hours (or days in the case of cricket!) When it comes to supporting a particular team, there is a sense of community, the unity of gathering around a specific cause, and the feeling of being part of something bigger. There is the thrill of not knowing what is going to happen or how it is ultimately going to make us feel. There are the extremes of emotions—either disappointment or joy, each to greater or lesser degrees depending on who you support!

Watching sports, like enjoying music and drama and many other good gifts of God, is a gift given to help us understand more of the God who made this world and to ultimately cause us to delight in him and the world he has made.

The communal aspect of fandom is an integral part of this gift. Whether it's mingling with other parents on the sideline of a youth game, watching at home on the sofa with friends or singing with thousands of others in a stadium, being a fan can be an incredibly unifying experience.

As we saw in the last chapter, Nelson Mandela famously reflected on the healing powers of sports in a country, as South Africa united around its rugby union team when it hosted the Rugby World Cup in 1995, by saying that it "has the power to change the world ... to unite people ... [to] create hope." Mandela was overstating it, but in essence he was right. Since we are made in the image of a fundamentally relational God, the unity and community that sports bring as we watch with others—who, apart from their love of that sport, may not be like us at all—can be a small glimpse into how we were truly made to be, and how it will be for God's people in eternity—as people from every background, tribe and tongue all worship God together.

Whether someone is a follower of Jesus or not, there is real joy to be found in the communal singing, the focus on a shared experience and the joy that can be experienced with others when watching sports. All of these are gifts of common grace—gifts given by God to all people regardless of their relationship with him: "He has shown kindness by giving you rain from heaven and crops in their seasons; he provides you with plenty of food and fills your hearts with joy" (Acts 14:17). The explosion of joy in the stands when a team scores the game-winner is literally a gift from God.

But not only that: it is a signpost from God. The rootedness of being a fan within a specific community and being in a place where, though imperfectly, we can experience fellowship, joy, love and a sense of place can point towards the rootedness that believers will experience in the world to come (Hebrews 11:16). They are a sign pointing towards how we are truly made to be: part of God's great "fan club," worshiping him for eternity.

Whether it's in the stadium or on the sofa with friends, next time you are cheering on your team and you experience that sense of camaraderie, of excitement, of joy, of being part of something much bigger than yourself, pause and do two things. First, thank God for this gift to you of this moment with these people. And second, think to yourself, "This is just a glimmer of what heaven will be like"—and thank God for that, too!

The Danger

Like all good gifts, our team and the experience of supporting it are gifts given to point to the giver of the gifts and not to be worshiped themselves. It is so easy to get this wrong. As Nick Hornby put it in his classic autobiographical book on his passionate lifelong support of Arsenal, the EPL team:

> *"As I get older, the tyranny that [soccer] exerts over my life, and therefore over the lives of people around me, is less reasonable and less attractive. Family and friends know, after long years of wearying experience, that the fixture list always has the last word in any arrangement; they understand, or at least accept, that [baptisms] or weddings*

> *or any gatherings, which in other families would take unquestioned precedence, can only be plotted after consultation. So [soccer] is regarded as a given disability that has to be worked around. If I were wheelchair-bound, nobody close to me would organise anything in a top-floor flat, so why would they plan anything for a winter Saturday afternoon?"* [62]

We've seen already how sports can be used as a god-substitute and become where we look for what is meant to be found in God alone: our ultimate joy, our deepest identity and even our functional salvation. When it comes to supporting a team, this is sometimes not even particularly subtle. We can so easily replace God with our fandom, and it is not hard to find someone who describes their support of their team as like a religion. We attend our place of worship, we praise our gods, we unite for the cause, we sing our songs of belonging, and we allow our emotions (not just for 90 minutes but for the whole weekend and on into the week) to be directed by how our idols perform.

Nick Hornby is describing what happens when a good thing becomes an ultimate thing. It destroys. While the unpredictable nature of sports make them fun to watch, it also makes it a horrible place to look to for our identity and joy consistently. It is a good gift and a bad god. "The tyranny" soccer "exerts ... is less reasonable and less attractive," he writes—but notice that he then goes on to excuse his decision to be dictated to by the demands of his god (Arsenal).

Paul is talking about this in Romans 1 when he says:

For although they knew God, they neither glorified him as God nor gave thanks to him ... They exchanged the truth about God for a lie, and worshiped and served created things rather than the Creator.

(Romans 1:21, 25)

The challenging point is this: it is possible even for Christians to worship their team rather than their Creator.

It might not be a team but a particular player. Athletes are some of the biggest celebrities and highest earners. Younger generations are moving away from more traditional support of teams and towards following individual sports stars more, so that whoever the biggest stars play for, that is who they'll support. The most followed accounts on Instagram are not teams but players. While there is obviously nothing wrong with liking someone and following them (especially if their character is one to be praised and imitated), we need to be wary of this slipping into idolatry—of our fandom becoming worship.

So, whether for us it's LA Lakers or Toronto Maple Leafs or Patrick Mahomes or Caitlin Clark, we need to check our hearts. How do we know if the sport or team or particular athlete that we love is becoming a potential idol?

It has often been said that you can see what someone truly worships by looking at their cash and their calendar. A story is told of two fans of the University of Alabama's football team. The couple purchased a

$300,000 campervan to attend games, and they were so obsessed that they even missed their daughter's wedding because it clashed with a match.[63] That is worship.

Closer to home, I (Jonny) still vividly remember my mother gently leaning over me as a church gathering was about to begin, and encouraging me to put my phone away as I frantically refreshed to see the latest cricket score.

It's helpful to ask some key questions of ourselves:

- Would I be more excited about my team winning a game on a Saturday or someone being baptized at my church on a Sunday?

- What takes precedence in how I spend my money and my time? Would I be more likely to give up buying a ticket to support a missionary or the other way round? Am I more likely to miss reading the Bible on a Saturday or 15 minutes of the game on TV?

- Am I open to challenge about my fandom, or do I tend to ignore people who "just don't get it" and find reasons to justify the decisions I've made?

The Power of the Tongue

With the tongue we praise our Lord and Father, and with it we curse human beings, who have been made in God's likeness. Out of the same mouth come praise and cursing. My brothers and sisters, this should not be.
(James 3:9-10)

Perhaps the biggest challenge for us as Christians watching our team is the way we use our words. How easy it is to forget that the players and fans of a rival team—and the referee—are made in God's image. How easy it is to think nothing of singing crude chants, booing opponents, piling in on the criticism of the players and uniting with the rest of the stadium in abusing the officials, and then the next day singing songs of praise to God at church. This should feel incongruous to us.

Those we speak about are fellow humans, made in the image of God. Be in no doubt that our words affect those we abuse. Former Arsenal player Gilberto Silva found the abuse so intolerable that he co-founded an app—Striver—that a number of elite athletes are encouraged to use to help deal with the abuse they get. He played in an era before social media became as critical as it is today, and yet still he remembers:

> *"People came onto my social media and smashed me with all the terrible comments you can imagine. I closed the comments and the apps and had a little peace, but they still ran in my mind."* [64]

Whether it's online, in the stands, or sitting with friends discussing the game in a bar, we need to remember that as those with a new identity, we are called to speak, Paul tells us, "only what is helpful for building others up according to their needs, that it may benefit those who listen" (Ephesians 4:29). It's challenging to think that we might be pretty silent in a conversation if we were to take this to heart. We need to acknowledge that so often we are guilty of slander, gossip and trolling, and to pray that God would transform our speech with truth and love (v 25, 32).

Meanwhile, back with James, he goes on to challenge his readers in their use of their tongue by outlining what our conduct and words are to look like:

The wisdom that comes from heaven is first of all pure; then peace-loving, considerate, submissive, full of mercy and good fruit, impartial and sincere. Peacemakers who sow in peace reap a harvest of righteousness. (James 3:17-18)

Today our tongue includes what we type, text, post and sign. What would it look like to be someone who is pure and peace-loving in your speech? What would it look like to be distinctive in your words about others when you're discussing a game with your friends or sitting in front of the TV with your kids?

There is grace for all we get wrong in this area. We need a Saviour, and we have one—and we need his Spirit to help us, and we have him. Perhaps you need to pause now to repent, to ask for forgiveness, and to ask him to show you and strengthen you to be very different next time the referee gets a penalty decision wrong, or the opposition score, or your team's newest player—who in your opinion should not have been signed—makes a big mistake.

Another Chance to Pray, Play, Say Together

As much as for those involved in competing in sports, being a fan is an opportunity to witness to Jesus in our prayerful, thoughtful conduct and speech with those we spend time with each week. Sporting teams are often places which knit together our towns and communities. It's crucial, as Christians on mission, that we don't ignore these places. Jesus told his followers, "You are the salt of the earth [and] the light of the world" (Matthew 5:13-14) and to "let your light shine before others" (v 16). The preserving and flavoring work of Christians as "salt" and our brightening work as "the light of the world" is to be a blessing to others, which includes those in stadiums and on sidelines.

Ultimately, we shine as we illuminate Christ for people—as we show in how we live and speak what he is like, praying that they would come to love and glorify him too. This will mean living differently—showing that there's something (well, someone) more exciting than any team or player. It will mean praying for those you sit and watch with. And it probably means being deliberate in deepening your sporting friendships, so that you talk about more than just the sport. Next time you're sitting in the stands before a match or traveling to an away game, ask those around you about their life outside of sports—how they're doing, how work is going, how their family are, what they're worried about. It may take a while for the barriers to come down, but in time they will. There are real opportunities to build deep and genuine friendships with those you regularly watch sports with.

Living as a Christian supporter will look different for each of us, of course. But it can't mean leaving our Christian convictions and identity at the front door as we head to the game, or forgetting what and who we most love whenever we turn the TV on. Let your supporting be a gift from God to be enjoyed, a signpost from God to point towards the glories of heaven, and an opportunity to love others, live distinctively, and share Jesus when you can.

Chapter 8

A Word for... Parents

"It started with the local team when the coach said she had potential. Not only that: I could tell she loved to play. Little did we know this was the beginning of an exciting but daunting journey into a completely different world for both of us. There is now a training session every day and regular trips up and down the country. We're always squeezing in homework, church seems to have slipped down the priority list, and socializing with friends is non-existent... and it's not just her!"

"As a parent, I often feel like a taxi service. Housework gets left undone, church and home group are increasingly hard to attend, and spending time with family and friends now needs a place in the diary! But I do love it..."

Do either of these stories sound familiar to some extent? Whether your child is on an elite performance pathway or playing for a local rec team, there can be similar challenges... but you do love it. Your child loves their sports, and so do you.

There are immense joys in walking with a child on their journey in sports: watching them improve, succeed and push themselves; seeing them interact with their peers and their coaches. But there are also the lows: frustration and tempers rising when games don't go as expected or they benched; family tension as one child feels they get less attention than another; facing decisions around whether to go to church or a game, how much sports is too much, and so on.

And in every moment, the good and the slightly less good, you have opportunities to teach your children and point them to Jesus as they see how you act and react. What do you say when your child loses? When they win? When they've been benched? When something needs to take precedence over practice or a game?

What Matters Most

Our primary role as parents is to lead our children towards God and show them how to keep him central in our lives. Our responsibility is to teach them the supremacy of Christ in all things (Colossians 1:18) and "the surpassing worth of knowing Jesus [our] Lord" (Philippians 3:8), and this includes his supremacy and worth in and over our sports.

We need to be explicit here. We are called as parents to raise our children to know Jesus (as far as we are able to) more than we are tasked with helping them be the best athletes they can be. Better unfulfilled sporting potential and a life lived trusting Jesus than the other way around. Deuteronomy 6:5-7 instructs us:

Love the LORD your God with all your heart and with all your soul and with all your strength. These commandments that I give you today are to be on your hearts. Impress them on your children. Talk about them when you sit at home and when you walk along the road, when you lie down and when you get up.

We are to impress Jesus on our children—to talk about him when we sit at home, when we drive to and from games, when we process wins and losses, and when we explain why we've decided to not do this or to do that. Sports offer us moments when we can share joys and sadness together and help our children process these emotions.

Karen, a mom of two sporty children, recognized this aspect of her parenting:

"It's a great opportunity to spend time with your children in that environment and hopefully then show them how you can be very competitive, how you can enjoy sports, but that it isn't everything. To show them how you can share faith and sports and it can all be interconnected." [65]

We Can Point Our Children to Jesus... *Through Helping Our Kids Place Sports in its Right Place*

As one dad, Richard, puts it:

"Winning matters, but not as much as I often think it does as a competitive person. It's challenging to work

through that with a Christian perspective, especially when as a parent you're one stage removed—you're not the competitor. I need to be a supportive parent without going too far and becoming the overbearing, irritating dad!" [66]

As we've seen but often struggle to remember, sports are a good gift from God that can be played for his glory and our good. And yet it is just that—a good gift. One of the big discussions parents and children need to have together (and one of the most important things parents can model to their children) is about its rightful place in our lives.

In 1 Corinthians 9:25, Paul reminds us that...

everyone who competes in the games goes into strict training. They do it to get a crown that will not last; but we do it [that is, we keep living with Christ Jesus as our Savior and Lord] to get a crown that will last for ever.

As parents make decisions about their children's involvement in sports, they could look at a verse like this and withdraw them from sports altogether. It can be hard to juggle school, sports, family life and church—and so it seems that the obvious response is not to let our children get involved in organized sports. And indeed, this may be the best decision for you and your family.

But it doesn't *have* to mean that. Paul is not saying that it's wrong or unhelpful to be someone who competes and trains for a crown that will not last. He's saying that it's wrong to let that kind of crown cause you to forget about the one that *will* last. It's about priorities and remembering what matters most.

So here's a diagnostic question we need to regularly be asking: what do we want most for our children—and are our decisions bearing out our answer to that question?

Would we rather our child became an elite athlete (or just someone better than most other children in their school) or that they learned that there are some non-negotiables as a family and sports fit around these? This is not an easy conversation to have as parents (and then as families), but keep talking through decisions about your time and your parenting. You might well find it helpful to ask for wisdom from your church leaders—those whom the Lord has given to shepherd you.

We Can Point Our Children to Jesus... *Through Not Leaving Discipleship to the Coach*

You are always discipling your children—either towards seeing Jesus as of surpassing worth or away from that. No parenting act is neutral. A conversation with an adult athlete underlined this for us. She said, "I felt loved by my parents when I was winning, so in the end I was striving to perform and win on the sole basis of being accepted and loved by my family." How sad—and yet how close to home this could be for us. It's very possible that those parents didn't set out to suggest that their love was based on sporting achievement—but that's how they came across. And of course, if our children feel that parental love grows or diminishes according to their success and failings, they are going to struggle to appreciate that God is a God of grace, whose love for his children is unchanging.

Not only is it easy for us to make our love and approval seem to rely on sporting success; it can also be very easy for us to project our own hopes and dreams onto our children. Maybe we long for our child to do what we couldn't do ourselves—to succeed in ways we never did. Or maybe we link our performance as a parent to our children's performance on the field. Both are making an idol of our children's success, and both will burden our children unfairly. You just need to spend a few minutes on the sideline of a youth football game to see this play out.

Another mom, Sally, realized how important it was to remind her children of their secure identity both in Christ and within the family:

> "I think what you consider success or even what you consider as failure can be different when you have a Christian faith because you're not defined by results and achievements and what trophies may or may not be on your mantelpiece. That actually I am defined by what God says about me. And I think really that's what we've tried to show our children." [67]

What you say to your children in victory and defeat, in joy and disappointment, and how you help them process their emotions in those times, really matters. They are wonderful opportunities to speak about the gospel in a rich and relevant way. We need to listen to ourselves and see if we only praise our children when they perform well, and instead be on the lookout to praise their care for a teammate or their reaction in the face of disappointment. Praise character more than ability.

Remember, too, that you are the parent and not the coach. First, this means the coach is someone in authority, who is to be treated with respect (whether or not you think you'd do a better job!). Second, coaches will generally base their decisions and their approval on performance, but as parents our love is unconditional. Sally notes how she needs "to remember that I am mum; I'm not the coach, I'm not the athlete. I am mum at the end of the day. And I will always be there, whatever the ups and the downs." And so will God.

One thing sports teaches children is how to lose. Sports are littered with disappointment and is a wonderful training ground for greater challenges in life to come. It is one of the reasons why we would argue strongly for the opportunity for our children to lose and, as they get into their teenage years, to be benched if the coach feels that is the right decision. But as parents, it can be tempting to want to shield our children from failure and adversity. Yet as Christians, we know that we are limited, fallible creatures and that this is a fallen world. We also know that trials and hardships are a way that God grows us to be more like Jesus. Much as we may wish it were not so, our children's lives will be marked by difficulties as well as delights—and playing sports when they are young is a great field in which to train them in how to navigate these things well and with a biblical worldview.

We Can Point our Children to Jesus... *Through Making the Most of Every Opportunity*

As we intentionally build friendships with other parents, serve the team through washing kit without complaint, support the coach when everyone else is criticizing them, and so on, we make the most of every opportunity that parenting in sports brings not only to point our children to Jesus but to point everyone else who is involved to him too.

There are countless ways to serve in a sports environment and many opportunities to build relationships with people you may otherwise not have met. Your conduct and speech as a parent can be a radical witness to those on the sidelines with you. From deliberately speaking well of the organization of the team or the performance of others to trying to get to know people outside of the sporting context, the stand and the sidelines are a rich mission field.

Some of us will be natural at starting up conversations as we watch our children run, tackle, kick and so on. Most of us will find it hard! One helpful framework to keep in your head is...

- *Your news:* Ask parents about their family and their work and their own hobbies. Show a real interest in them and try to get to know the rhythms of their lives. In time, they may ask you similar questions.

- *My news:* When you are asked such questions, look for natural ways to speak about your faith in Jesus. Can you mention your church and what a significant impact it has on you each week?

- *Good news:* As you become more intentional in your relationships, very often you will have an opportunity to share a little about the good news of Jesus. Look for church events you can invite parents to or simply carve out deliberate time with them both as parents and as a whole family—carpool, have meals together on the road, or invite them to spend time in your family home.

We can Point Our Children to Jesus...
By Remembering God's Grace in Our Lives

The best thing you and I can do for our children is to walk closely with Jesus ourselves. That can be a battle for all of us, so we need to be honest with ourselves here. A spouse or Christian friend can also help with accountability, and praying with them is essential. In fact, making sure you are prioritizing time with your spouse outside of ferrying children around is important.

Being a parent is a privilege, but it is not easy. In all of it, we need God's help! Remember that your own identity is not to be found in your children's achievement or even in their profession of faith but in being loved unconditionally as a child of our heavenly Father.

The pastor and author Paul Tripp reminds us that we do not parent in our own strength:

"We serve a gloriously loving and powerful Redeemer. He loves our children infinitely more than we do [and he] called you as a parent to be a humble and faithful tool of change in the lives of your children. And for that there is moment by moment grace." [68]

Praise for the Lord for his grace in our lives. Let dwelling on his love help you to point your children to him as you parent them through the ups and downs of sports.

Chapter 9

A Word About... Sports on Sundays

In any book about playing sports and following Christ, there is a topic that must be addressed, or it will keep nagging at you from page to page—what about Sunday sports and church? This is the chapter where we grasp that nettle!

While this is not a new question that Christians have had to think through, it has become a more prominent one as increasing numbers of professional and youth sports (which themselves are becoming more professional) take place on Sundays. Today, in many places, the general assumption among sports-loving Christians is that we will fit church around sports and not the other way round. According to a recent study published in the Review of Religious Research, when pastors of 16 US congregations experiencing declining attendance were interviewed, the most common reason cited for the decline was children's sport on Sunday.

The research did not establish if this was in fact the definitive reason, but the very fact that the headline has such traction implies that it is a factor and, to many, a concern. Another study looked at whether NFL home games affected church attendance in the cities those games were played in—and the result, overwhelmingly, was that they did.

So how, as Christians, at any level of sport, do we reflect on this and make faithful, godly and wise decisions?

A Disputable Matter

Deciding whether to play sports on a Sunday or not is a matter of conscience for each Christian. In Romans 14, Paul addresses the question of areas that Christians disagree over that are not central to the gospel—"disputable matters" (v 1):

> *One person considers one day more sacred than another; another considers every day alike. Each of them should be fully convinced in their own mind. Whoever regards one day as special does so to the Lord ... For none of us lives for ourselves alone, and none of us dies for ourselves alone. If we live, we live for the Lord; and if we die, we die for the Lord. So, whether we live or die, we belong to the Lord. (v 5-8)*

Note that Paul is not promoting a wishy-washy approach to our faith which says, *Just do what you want; it's all fine.* He is saying we all need to have our own thoughts and come to our own convictions when it comes to thinking about things such as holy days.

A few verses earlier, Paul has exhorted the church to not fall out with others who hold different convictions on these "disputable matters," but he still calls us to consider them carefully.

So how do we navigate a conscience issue like this?

1. *Listen to your conscience and then follow it.* We are to be "fully convinced" in our own minds and then to act on that. We are to do this even when other Christians might come to a different position from ours.

2. *Whichever position you currently hold, listen to wise Christians* and be willing to accept your conscience might be wrong. The verses here don't give permission for a stubborn refusal to admit you may have something wrong.

3. *Honor others' consciences by supporting their decisions* and doing all you can not to encourage them to go against their consciences. Paul goes into this in more detail in 1 Corinthians 8:9-13, where he says it's better not to do something you consider yourself free to do if, in doing so, you encourage another Christian to follow your example and do something that their conscience is telling them is wrong to do.

Those are the principles to bear in mind as you think through this particular issue, which is not all-important (it's not about our salvation) but equally is not unimportant (because we want to please God in all that we do). In the rest of this chapter, we'll outline what we think and where we have landed on this issue of Sunday sports—not necessarily to try to persuade you but to show you how some people view this issue as you think and pray it through yourself.

The Sabbath Day Today

In the Old Testament, keeping the Sabbath was a key identity marker for God's people as well as a key part of their obedience to God's covenant—it's the fourth commandment (Exodus 20:8-11). But does this command carry forward into the New Testament after the coming of Jesus and the sending of the Spirit?

Christians happily accept that there are many aspects of the Old Testament law which are not markers of faithfulness today—for instance, the food laws (Mark 7:19) and the temple sacrificial system (Hebrews 10:1-7). Other aspects still very much apply—for instance the command to love your neighbor or to honor your marriage (Leviticus 19:18 and Matthew 22:37-40; Exodus 20: 14 and Hebrews 13:4).

So, what about the Sabbath commandment? In Colossians 2:16-17 Paul writes:

> Do not let anyone judge you by what you eat or drink, or with regard to a religious festival, a New Moon celebration or a Sabbath day. These are a shadow of the things that were to come; the reality, however, is found in Christ.

Paul seems to be saying here that keeping a Sabbath is not something that is a matter of obedience to God now any more than what we eat. Why? Because "these" laws were pointing towards the spiritual reality that we enjoy in Christ. Observing the Sabbath in the ways that the Old Testament stipulated was a shadow of things to come.

Consequently, our view is that Christians can be flexible about it. But again, a key thing to remember, which Paul is teaching us in both Colossians 2 and Romans 14, is not to be judgmental when others have different opinions on it:

> *Let us stop passing judgment on one another.*
> *Instead, make up your mind not to put any stumbling*
> *block or obstacle in the way of a brother or sister.*
> *(Romans 14:13)*

And, while we take the view that Jesus' coming changed the way God's people approach the Sabbath, there are still key commands given to God's people that will shape how we think about our Sundays: commands about gathering as church and having a day of rest.

Here are three biblical principles to reflect on.

1. WE WERE CREATED TO REST

In Genesis 2, right at the beginning of the Bible, we see God resting on and blessing the seventh day:

> *By the seventh day God had finished the work he had*
> *been doing; so on the seventh day he rested from all*
> *his work. Then God blessed the seventh day and made*
> *it holy, because on it he rested from all the work of*
> *creating that he had done. (v 2-3)*

It's incredible to think that God, who needs no rest, rested. Made in his image, we are called to rest too.

Unlike God, we are creatures with limitations, and we do all need to rest. We know this from our sporting lives: rest and recovery days are essential even when we are in a period of heavy training. But biblical rest is not only (or even primarily) about physical rest. In Matthew 11:29, Jesus tells us that true rest is found in him:

Take my yoke upon you and learn from me, for I am gentle and humble in heart, and you will find rest for your souls.

Hebrews 4 then tells us that *spiritual* rest is available now, through trusting in Christ's death and resurrection for salvation and enjoying his presence and forgiveness day by day as we walk towards our heavenly home with him.

Rest, then, is not just about stopping work; it is also about enjoying time to focus on God and find refreshment in him. It is to respond to Jesus' invitation to "Come to me ... and I will give you rest" (Matthew 11:28).

So, wherever you end up landing on Sunday sports, ask yourself: am I obeying God's call and invitation to rest—and am I enabling my family to do so as well?

2. WE CAN WORSHIP GOD 24/7

We don't need to dwell on this here as the whole of this book has looked at how all parts of our lives, including our sports, can be acts of worship. There is a church in London which has a big sign above its door as you walk out which reads, "Now go and worship." Paul in

Romans 12 reminds us that our worship is not just confined to a church meeting or church activity on a particular day—our "true and proper worship" is to "offer [our] bodies as a living sacrifice" in response to God's mercy (v 1).

3. WE WERE MADE TO MEET TOGETHER

If you took these two principles on their own, you could end up playing sports every Sunday and chilling on the sofa on a Monday. But this would ignore the fact that the Christian life is never to be lived alone. God, in his very being as Father, Son and Spirit, has always been in relationship, and we have been made in his image. We need each other as we live in this life.

So while we want to argue that the law has been fulfilled and that rest and worship are now 24/7, we also want to underline how easy it can be to miss the importance of the corporate gathering of God's people of all ages and stages, in a particular place, each week, to worship him together. It may not be too strong to say that the single most important thing believers can do is meet together with other Christians to sit under God's word and participate in the sacraments.

The New Testament recognizes that it is possible for believers to consider giving up on meeting together:

And let us consider how we may spur one another on towards love and good deeds, not giving up meeting together, as some are in the habit of doing, but encouraging one another—and all the more as you see the Day approaching. (Hebrews 10:24-25)

When this was written, Christians were beginning to face persecution—and so there would have been a strong temptation to simply give up on the risky activity of meeting together in person. Yet the message is clear—even though these believers might risk their lives in doing so, they're not to give up meeting together. Why? Because we need other Christians, and they need us, and without meeting to worship God together, it is very hard for us to run our race of faith.

Think of a marathon—the encouragement of fellow runners and the cheers of the supporters help spur you on to the finish line. Church is wonderful, and vital for all Christians. As we meet, sit under the teaching of God's word, sing and pray and smile and weep together, and as we take communion and practice baptism, we are encouraged to keep trusting Jesus and to keep going in godly living. We do this together with others— some who are like us and some who are very unlike us, some who are sporty and some who are totally not— showcasing the diversity of the body of Christ to all who come (and, indeed, to the heavenly realms—Ephesians 3:10-11). We were made to meet, and we need to meet, week by week.

So while the Sabbath command may no longer be in place, the command to meet for corporate worship as God's people, under his word, remains.

So, ask yourself: am I or my family in danger of allowing sporting commitments to prevent us from obeying the command to meet together and to encourage one another?

So, What Do I *Do*?!

In a sense, this question is more straightforward for the professional athletes to answer. Playing on a Sunday is their job and part of their contracts. Their position is similar to other shift workers such as doctors and police officers. Nevertheless, being part of a local church is essential for elite athletes, even if they cannot always (or even often) attend on a Sunday.

The former Great Britain Olympics rower Debbie Flood reflects on the importance of this as she looks back on her career:

> *"When I was away on training camp or competing, it was important to know that my church was praying for me—that they were in contact with me. I had a prayer partner from church who was messaging regularly to ask how I was getting on, but also challenging me, asking if I was reading my Bible, encouraging me to enjoy growing in my personal relationship with Jesus."*[69]

Meeting as a whole community, of all ages, backgrounds and interests, to worship God and encourage each other is the unique opportunity of the Sunday service as we hear God's word taught and share in the Lord's Supper together. If, however, you do need to miss a Sunday, make it more of a priority to meet up with others in the week. If you are away for a period due to the nature of your sport (and this mainly affects elite athletes), then ask someone in your church to pray for you and ask you how you're doing.

Things are different for amateur competitors and

children, where it is not a job but (however seriously we take it) a choice. Perhaps the major challenge is that many amateur games or races are now held on Sunday mornings.

Of course, some people are members of churches whose meeting time happens not to clash with their sporting fixtures. But where that is not the case, since attending church is pivotal to the Christian life, how can this dilemma be solved?

Some people simply stop playing in order to attend church regularly. Others seek to find a team or a league which plays on a Saturday or a Sunday afternoon.

Others keep playing, but approach their sport differently because they are followers of Jesus and their sport happens on a Sunday.

For instance, Gill Bland, as a marathon runner with a young family, faces this challenge:

> *"Growing up, my parents brought me up with a real strong ethos of Sunday services coming first. This wasn't a legalistic point of view, but it was really helpful because it has helped me frame things in the right way and has shaped how I approach it now as a runner when lots of races are on Sundays. So now there are times when we've had to say as a family that we won't do a race to stop us missing a number of Sundays in a row."* [70]

Adults must work out what they see the Bible teaching in this area, and how their conscience is directing them, and then weigh up their options. For children, the responsibility lies with their parents. There is no doubt that deciding to prioritize meeting with God's people and the decisions that then causes about when to go to church or whether to move church has caused tension and difficulty in thousands of Christian homes in recent times. Our advice would be to work out what is right for you in terms of following Jesus and obeying him; then work out what that means for you as a family, including if any changes need to be made; and then talk openly and clearly about that with your children. Make sure that they know *why* you're acting as you are. Of course they may not agree, but you can pray that you showing them that Jesus comes first (however that looks for your family) will be used by the Lord to bring them to faith or grow them in their faith.

In all these decisions, a conversation with the church leadership is essential. It is worth saying that as authors, we are not your pastors. Your pastors or elders may have wisdom you haven't thought of and will be able to speak into your situation. So do talk with them about it and be open to hearing what they have to say as your leaders. Invite them to challenge you and to keep you accountable if they feel you are not prioritizing both rest and meeting together with other believers. We're usually very good at justifying to ourselves the decisions that make our lives easier or more comfortable! We need to let Christian friends and our church leaders ask us the hard questions around our priorities.

You may agree with all or most of what we've said here—or you may land in a very different place when it comes to how to honor God with your Sundays. That's fine. We hope we've given you more of a framework for thinking this through biblically and wisely than we have simply given you our position. So as we close, we'd encourage you to ask yourself these four questions, prayerfully and carefully, and be willing to live out where the Spirit and your conscience lead you:

- How can I best obey God's call to rest and enable my family to as well?

- How might I be in danger (or how might we as a family be in danger) of allowing sporting commitments to cause me not to obey the command to meet together with God's people?

- Does my behavior in this area show to myself and others that gathering together with Christians on a Sunday is supremely important to me for my spiritual health and that of my family? Does anything need to change?

- Am I being loving, humble and encouraging of those who take a different approach in this area?

Chapter 10

A Word for... Coaches

"A coach will impact more young people in a year than the average person does in a lifetime."
Billy Graham

Without coaches and managers there is no competitive sports. We don't need coaches to play with friends in the park or go for a run on our own, but to see any improvement, we need the help of someone with expertise to encourage and develop our skills.

If you have children who get involved in sports teams, it is likely that you'll be asked to coach at some point. This is often how people first get started in amateur sports—and it's a great opportunity to be a real influence in the lives of young people. At the elite level, the same principles apply—you just need more experience and qualifications, and a certain level of coaching ability, to perform at that level.

So, just as we asked when it came to supporting a

team, the question is: how can I coach in a distinctly *Christian* way?

Competence

Whatever your hand finds to do, do it with all your might. (Ecclesiastes 9:10)

You may have expected the first point to be about godly character (and we'll get there), but first and foremost it is important that you are capable at the technical, tactical and management sides of coaching. To serve a team and its players well, it is vital to coach proficiently.

Coaching is an opportunity to use God-given talents to serve players God has placed in our care. To coach a team or individual is an opportunity to serve our community and so it is a responsibility to which we should commit. This means we may need to go on coaching courses to develop, and we'll need to make sure the logistics for the team are organized efficiently and be clear in how we communicate.

Jane Powell has coached all over the world and at the highest level, having originally been a PE teacher in her local school. Excellence is her key principle as a Christian coach:

"Everything should be done with excellence because we're doing it to for God. We're not doing it for men; we're not doing it for coaches. We're doing it to say, 'Thank you, because you've given me these abilities, and I want to give them back to you, and I want to be the best I can be because of what you've given me'."[71]

When God calls us to serve others with our creative and relational skills, he expects us to take that seriously. As Paul writes to the Colossians, "Whatever you do, work at it with all your heart, as working for the Lord" (Colossians 3:23). Whether your coaching is a voluntary role or salaried employment, give the role your very best, working "with all your heart"—not to receive praise and glory from those we coach or the parents who watch but to please our Lord.

Character

College basketball coach John Wooden is known as one of the greatest coaches of all time. He was also a Christian. He became famous for his "Woodenisms"—catchy phrases which have become mantras for many coaches. One of his most famous ones is about character:

> "Be more concerned with your character than your reputation, because your character is what you really are, while your reputation is merely what others think you are."[72]

In other words, care more about being godly in what you do than in what others think of you. A Christian coach will aim to be distinctly Christian in their attitudes and behavior. It's worth reading a passage like this one from Colossians 3 in terms of how to coach "with all your heart, as working for the Lord":

> Now you must also rid yourselves of all such things as these: anger, rage, malice, slander, and filthy language from your lips. Do not lie to each other, since you have taken off your old self with its practices and have put

on the new self, which is being renewed in knowledge in the image of its Creator. (v 8-10)

Ask yourself:

- *When it comes to anger and rage:* How do you respond to mistakes your team makes? How do you react when a player deliberately ignores your instructions?

- *In terms of slander, filthy language and lies:* How do you speak about the players you coach? How do you speak to them?

These are things to "take off"—they belong to our old non-Christian selves. Then look at what Paul commands us to put on:

As God's chosen people, holy and dearly loved, clothe yourselves with compassion, kindness, humility, gentleness and patience. Bear with each other and forgive one another if any of you has a grievance against someone. Forgive as the Lord forgave you. And over all these virtues put on love, which binds them all together in perfect unity. (v 12-14)

How striking it is to meet a technically excellent coach who also displays all these qualities. A person who, while striving for excellence and being firm in their decision-making, still treats everyone with compassion and kindness.

Coaching can be a difficult and tense job as you manage people with a variety of expectations. It is hard to tell a player that they have not been selected on a team, and it is demanding to treat everyone with dignity and empathy.

The ability to exercise these characteristics is God-given. It is based upon remembering that you are "holy and dearly loved" by God because of your faith in Christ, not because of how well (or not!) your coaching goes. It is enhanced by viewing players as people—human beings with profound emotions.

Everyone you coach is a person first, a player second. Jurgen Klopp, who coached the Premier League soccer team Liverpool from 2015–2024, and won the EPL in 2020 and the European Champions League the year before, is a Christian, and has regularly spoken about this. He was once stunned to find that a member of staff had no idea that the team's new signing, Andy Robertson, had just become a father. He challenged them, "How can you not know that? That's the biggest thing in his life now. Come on!"

As we reflected earlier regarding the experience of players, God will use the ups and downs of coaching to refine your character and chip away at your rough edges. The Holy Spirit will use the specific challenges and opportunities of coaching increasingly to form you into the likeness of Jesus. Even when a person has attained the highest level of coaching qualifications at the most prestigious sporting institutions, the ultimate educational establishment for the Christian is the school of discipleship. It is here that God uses your gift as a coach to mold and shape you into the likeness of Jesus Christ.

What a joy and privilege it is to have God change our lives and then to find ourselves capable of playing a positive role in molding the competence and character of those we coach!

Conviction

To increase in competence and develop our character, we must have the conviction that coaching is a good, God-honoring activity, rather than a neutral indulgence of our God-given time. We need to be assured that God is committed to the investment of time in coaching.

Paul concludes his message to the Colossians in a way that can be applied to our consideration of coaching sports:

And whatever you do, whether in word or deed, do it all in the name of the Lord Jesus, giving thanks to God the Father through him. (v 17)

In every aspect of coaching, in the things we do and say, we are representing Jesus. May we remember these profound truths of Christian discipleship and give thanks to God for the opportunity to shape the lives of young and old through the influence of being a coach.

And, by the way, you may find that you really enjoy coaching. You may even find yourself thinking that you could go on coaching others after you've coached your own children. Furthermore, you may find yourself thinking that the privilege of being a competent coach can, alongside the opportunity to form character in those you coach, enhance your conviction to be a coach, perhaps a lifelong coach.

Think about it like this. For most of us, there will be a limit on how long we can play whatever the sport is that forms a large part of our young adult lives. Age, injury and lack of time to keep fit enough to perform quite naturally lead to the end of a playing career. Coaching offers the prospect of being in the sports community for the rest of your adult life. It offers the prospect of lifelong relationships at your sports team as you continue to coach others in your sport. What an opportunity for the Christian to build community and to serve others in the name of Jesus Christ in the most enjoyable of activities.

Chris Jones has coached rugby in South Wales for decades. For him his conviction comes from his own experience of making mistakes when he was younger:

> "I think back on my own wasted rugby career, and I just want to help others not go down the roads I went down and to fulfill their potential not just as rugby players but as the best people they can be. I love what I do. I believe this is where God wants me to be." [73]

Tom Osborne was coach and Athletic Director at the University of Nebraska. He sums it up really well:

> "I think the basic theme behind it all is that no matter what role you are in, you do have a chance to serve. You can honor God with whatever circumstances you have been given ... That is essentially what we are called to do—to honor him with how we serve other people. Hopefully, everybody can think about their role and how it applies to them." [74]

Christians at the heart of sporting institutions, who serve all those who play, can have marvelous friendships with neighbors in their communities and cities.

It does not matter what level you are coaching or contributing at. Here is just one example from a very non-elite level. Dickie Bird has played a number of roles for his local soccer team in Essex, UK, including becoming an assistant referee in his 40s when his son started to play. Spending a lot of his week around the team has allowed him to build deep and precious friendships. His gospel convictions are what have kept him going for over 40 years there:

> "Being involved in soccer all my playing career, and only coming to Christ when my playing days were over, I was keen, and still am, to give as many youngsters as possible the opportunities that I never had to hear the gospel, so that it would have an impact at an early age. I'm just an ordinary, everyday guy. I'm not academic, but God has given me the one gift that I have, sport, to reach out to people. I would love to encourage others, but most of all I would love the glory to go to God."

May we all have Dickie's heart for the gospel and love for sports into our old age!

This book has hopefully shaped some of your broader convictions around sports:

- Sports are a good gift from God that we can play and coach people for—for his glory and our pleasure.

- Sports are an unstable foundation on which to build our identity.

- Sports can become an idol if we don't keep them in their right place as a gift.

- Sports give wonderful opportunities to serve and love others.

- Sports are an excellent opportunity for us to model and represent our faith in Jesus to others.

All of these are relevant for the coach or administrator, who has more of an opportunity to shape the culture of a team than any individual player. How could you take that opportunity seriously and look to foster an environment in which your faith is evident, so that it becomes plausible for those you coach to consider what following Jesus might look like for themselves?

Endnotes

1   Nancy Guthrie, *Even Better Than Eden: Nine Ways the Bible's Story Changes Everything About Your Story* (Crossway, 2018), p. 63.

2   Anthony Hoekema, *Created in God's Image* (Eerdmans, 1986), p. 67.

3   Timothy Keller with Katherine Leary Alsdorf, *Every Good Endeavor: Connecting Your Work to God's Work* (Hodder, 2012), p. 59.

4   *The Last Dance* (Netflix), Episode 2.

5   Julian Linden, "Unrelenting pressure makes Ryder Cup irresistible," www.reuters.com/article/sports/unrelenting-pressure-makes-ryder-cup-irresistible-idUSDEE890045/ (accessed November 5, 2024).

6   Jeremy Treat, "More Than a Game: A Theology of Sport" in *Themelios* 40:3, thegospelcoalition.org/themelios/article/more-than-a-game-theology-of-sport (accessed November 5, 2024).

7   christiansinsport.org.uk/resources/e55-anastasia-chitty-the-team-gb-rower (accessed November 5, 2024).

8   Quoted in Graham Daniels and J. Stuart Weir, *Born to Play* (10Publishing, 2014), p. 17.

9   "Brady breaks silence on rehab," patriots.com/news/brady-breaks-silence-on-rehab-142461 accessed November 7, 2024).

10   christiansinsport.org.uk/resources/ep-24-gavin-peacock-newcastle-and-chelsea-midfielder (accessed November 5, 2024).

11   C.S. Lewis, *Mere Christianity* (HarperCollins, 2011), p. 122.

12   William Fotheringham, "Lance Armstrong on the attack and doping controversy enters final stage," theguardian.com/sport/2012/jun/16/lance-armstrong-drugs-tour-de-france (accessed November 5, 2024).

13   It is unclear when Ronaldo first said this.

14   Timothy Keller, *Counterfeit Gods* (John Murray Press, Kindle Edition), loc. 84.

15   "More Than a Game: A Theology of Sport" in *Themelios* 40:3.

16   christiansinsport.org.uk/resources/e57-rosie-woodbridge-eating-disorders-and-high-performance-sport/ (accessed November 11, 2024).

17   www.cbsnews.com/news/transcript-tom-brady-part-3/ (accessed June 3, 2024).

18   As above.

19   Sabrina B. Little, *The Examined Run: Why Good People Make Better Runners* (Oxford University Press, 2024), p. 87.

20   Shirl Hoffman, *Good Game: Christianity and the Culture of Sports* (Baylor University Press, 2010), p. 148.

21   https://theicec.com/wp-content/uploads/2023/07/ICEC-Press-Release-Report-Published-27.06.23.pdf (accessed November 5, 2024).

22   Michael Phelps with Alan Abrahamson, *No Limits: The Will to Succeed* (Free Press, 2008), p. 9.

23   Sarah Spain, "Serena has plenty to say, in victory or defeat," https://www.espn.com/espnw/news-commentary/story/_/id/7988442/ (accessed November 5, 2024).

24   Sam Allberry, *What God Has to Say About Our Bodies* (Crossway, 2012), p. 84.

25   C.H. Spurgeon, "The Fourfold Treasure," https://www.spurgeon.org/resource-library/sermons/the-fourfold-treasure/#flipbook/ (accessed November 5, 2024).

26   *Plugged In: Connecting your faith with what you watch, read, and play* (The Good Book Company, 2019), p. 55.

27   Joshua Doering, "Yankees closer Clay Holmes finding freedom as 'living sacrifice' for the Lord," sportsspectrum.com/sport/baseball/2024/05/14/yankees-clay-holmes-freedom-living-sacrifice (accessed November 7, 2024).

28   christiansinsport.org/uk/resources/ep-46-anna-
     tipton-paralympian-goal-ball-player (accessed
     November 5, 2024).

29   "Roger Federer to retire after Laver Cup in
     September," www.bbc.co.uk/sport/tennis/
     62911876 (accessed November 5, 2024).

30   Wayne Grudem, *Business for the Glory of God*
     (Crossway, 2003), p. 65.

31   "The Increase: Matt Forte—Leaning on God's
     Counsel," https://sportsspectrum.com/the-
     increase/2018/11/01/the-increase-matt-forte-
     leaning-on-gods-counsel/ (accessed November 7,
     2024).

32   Dalton Trigg, "Don Nelson on Scouting Dirk: 'Most
     Unbelievable Young Player," https://www.si.com/nba/
     mavericks/news/don-nelson-dallas-mavs-scouting-
     dirk-nowtizki-hall-of-fame-most-unbeliveable-young-
     player (accessed November 7, 2024).

33   christiansinsport.org/uk/resources/ep-19-
     adam-pengilly-winter-olympian-the-danger-of-
     worshipping-your-sport/ (accessed November 5,
     2024).

34   Sydney McLaughlin-Levrone, "How Sydney
     McLaughlin-Levrone Overcame Her Fear with Faith,"
     https://guideposts.org/positive-living/how-sydney-
     mclaughlin-levrone-overcame-her-fear-with-faith/
     (accessed November 7, 2024).

35   C.S. Lewis, *The Weight of Glory* (MacMillan), p 5.

36   *The Works of Jonathan Edwards, Vol. 17: Sermons and Discourses, 1730-1733* (Yale University Press, 2000), p. 437-438.

37   Andre Agassi, *Open: An Autobiography* (HarperCollins, 2009), p. 26.

38   As above, p. 55.

39   As above, p. 166.

40   Dr. Carline Heaney, quoted in "Kadeena Cox and Esme Morgan on the mental impact of injuries," www.bbc.co.uk/sport/64895858 (accessed November 5, 2024).

41   Andy Bull, "Jonny Wilkinson: 'It took a few years for the pressure to really build. And then it exploded,'" www.theguardian.com/sport/2019/sep/08/jonny-wilkinson-mental-iilness-rugby-union (accessed June 3, 2024).

42   Matt Smethurst, "Fifty Quotes from Tim Keller (1950–2023)," thegospelcoalition.org/article/50-quotes-tim-keller (accessed November 5, 2024).

43   Ashley Null, "Reformation Care in the Olympic Village," in A. Parker, N.J. Watson & J. White (eds), *Sports Chaplaincy: Trends, Issues and Debates* (Routledge, 2016), p. 120-131.

44   Ashley Null, "Towards a Theology of Competitive Sport," *The Journal of the Christian Society of Kinesiology, Leisure and Sports Studies,* Volume 7, https://trace.tennessee.edu/cgi/viewcontent.cgi?article=1030&context=jcskls (accessed November 5, 2024).

45   Cole Claybourn, "Ministry? Coaching? Nick Foles seeks God's plan for life after football, whenever that time comes," https://sportsspectrum.com/sport/football/2022/02/22/ministry-coaching-nick-foles-gods-plan-football/ (accessed June 3, 2024).

46   Stuart Weir, "Nicola McDermott part 3—Nicola, God and Blanka," https://www.runblogrun.com/2021/07/nicola-mcdermott-part-3-nicola-god-and-blanka.html (accessed November 5, 2024).

47   Carey Lodge, "Olympian who helped competitor who fell: 'God prepared my heart to respond in that way,'" https://www.christiantoday.com/article/olympian.who.helped.competitor.who.fell.god.prepared.my.heart.to.respond.in.that.way/93410.htm (accessed November 5, 2024).

48   John Whitmore, *Coaching for Performance,* 4th edition (Nicholas Brealey Publishing, 2009), p. 10.

49   It is unclear when Jordan first said this.

50   Ashley Null, "Some Preliminary Thoughts on Philosophies of Sports Ministry and Their Literature," in Donald Deardorff II and John White (eds), *The Image of God in the Human Body* (Edwin Mellen Press, 2008), p. 247-248.

51   christiansinsport.org.uk/resources/ep-15-val-gin-american-volleyball-and-softball-coach-mentoring-the-next-generation (accessed November 5, 2024).

52   Michael Bamberger, "In rare rules decision, Russell
      Henley learned a lesson for all of us: call yourself on
      it!" https://golf.com/instruction/rules/russell-henley-
      learned-a-lesson-for-all-of-us/ (accessed November 7,
      2024).

53   Story first told in Graham Daniels and Stuart Weir,
      Born to Play (10Publishing, 2016), p. 68.

54   Quoted at www.globalgoals.org/news/sport-for-
      development-and-peace/ (accessed June 4, 2024).

55   Dick Lucas, *The Message of Colossians and Philemon*
      (IVP UK, 2000), p. 172.

56   Sam Chan, *How to Talk About Jesus (Without Being
      That Guy)* (Zondervan, 2020), p. 61.

57   www.youtube.com/watch?v=TqH_d2zo2PM (accessed
      November 11, 2024).

58   Dan Strange, *Making Faith Magnetic* (The Good Book
      Company, 2022), p. 158.

59   christiansinsport.org.uk/resources/e55-anastasia-
      chitty-the-team-gb-rower (accessed November 5,
      2024)

60   *How to Talk About Jesus (Without Being That Guy)*, p. 8.

61   christiansinsport.org.uk/resources/running-the-race-
      of-evangelism/ (accessed November 11, 2024).

62   Nick Hornby, *Fever Pitch* (Penguin, 2005), p. 212.

63   As told in Shirl Hoffman, *Good Game*, p. 1.

64   www.youtube.com/watch?v=SC_m5Kv8FoY (accessed
      June 4, 2024).

65   christiansinsport.org.uk/resources/ep-53-karen-
      kennedy-former-irish-hockey-international/
      (accessed November 11, 2024).

66   www.premiernexgen.com/helping-your-childs-faith-
      when-they-are-passionate-about-their-sport/16540.
      article (accessed November 11, 2024).

67   christiansinsport.org.uk/resources/life-as-a-mother-
      of-a-sport-mad-family/ (accessed November 11,
      2024).

68   Paul D. Tripp, *Parenting* (Crossway, 2016), p. 69-70.

69   christiansinsport.org.uk/resources/why-church-is-so-
      important-for-sportspeople/ (accessed November 11,
      2024).

70   christiansinsport.org.uk/resources/e65-gill-bland-
      the-marathon-runner/ (accessed November 11,
      2024).

71   christiansinsport.org.uk/resources/ep-10-jane-
      powell-england-cricket-and-hockey-player/ (accessed
      November 11, 2024).

72   Quoted in Walter Pavlo, "Character Is What You
      Do When EVERYONE Is Watching," Forbes.
      com, October 23, 2012, www.forbes.com/sites/
      walterpavlo/2012/10/23/character-is-what-you-do-
      when-everyone-is-watching/ (accessed November 6,
      2024).

73   christiansinsport.org.uk/resources/ep-16-chris-jones-coaching-as-a-christian-at-the-house-of-pain/ (accessed November 11, 2024).

74   Chris Carpenter, "Tom Osborne: Faith, Football & a Strong Foundation," https://cbn.com/article/not-selected/tom-osborne-faith-football-strong-foundation (accessed November 11, 2024).

BIBLICAL | RELEVANT | ACCESSIBLE

At The Good Book Company we are dedicated to helping Christians and local churches grow. We believe that God's growth process always starts with hearing clearly what he has said to us through his timeless and flawless word—the Bible.

Ever since we opened our doors in 1991, we have been striving to produce resources that are biblical, relevant, and accessible. By God's grace, we have grown to become an international publisher, encouraging ordinary Christians of every age and stage and every background and denomination to live for Christ day by day and equipping churches to grow in their knowledge of God, their love for one another, and the effectiveness of their outreach.

Call one of our friendly team for a discussion of your needs or visit one of our local websites for more information on the resources and services we provide.

Your friends at The Good Book Company